INVADERS AND SETTLERS
THE CELTS
A MASTER FILE

Editors

D C Perkins, BA (Hons), MEd, PhD (Wales) and E J Perkins, BSc (Hons), MEd

Illustrations by Anthony James

These Master Files are designed for use in the classroom. Each consists of teachers' notes, pupils' resource material, worksheets, activities and record sheet. Each book covers a part of the national curriculum in depth allowing the teacher to decide the amount of material to use according to the age and ability of the children.

DOMINO BOOKS (WALES) LTD
SWANSEA SA1 1 FN
Tel. 01792 459378   Fax. 01792 466337
The Celts Master File © EJP & DCP 1993 Reprinted 1994 (twice), 1995, 1996, 1997, 1998, 1999
ISBN 1 85772 067 9

CONTENTS

This book is planned to introduce pupils to the early history of the British Isles. It forms part of the National Curriculum for invaders and settlers - the Celts, Romans, Anglo-Saxons and Vikings.

NOTE TO TEACHERS

All the material in this book is photocopiable as defined on page 1. This means that all the material can be used in any way you wish in the classroom situation. It is intended that material be used at different levels depending on the ages and abilities of your pupils. Some worksheets may be used as colouring exercises or with the material below them as the basis for discussion or role play. Some of the worksheets and resources are more difficult and are intended for the older child. It may be possible to use some of the Teachers' Notes directly with more advanced and brighter students. We do not envisage any problems with selecting appropriate material. We hope you enjoy using this book and welcome any comments. There are other Domino Masterfiles on invaders and settlers (the Romans, Anglo Saxons and Vikings).

EJP and DCP

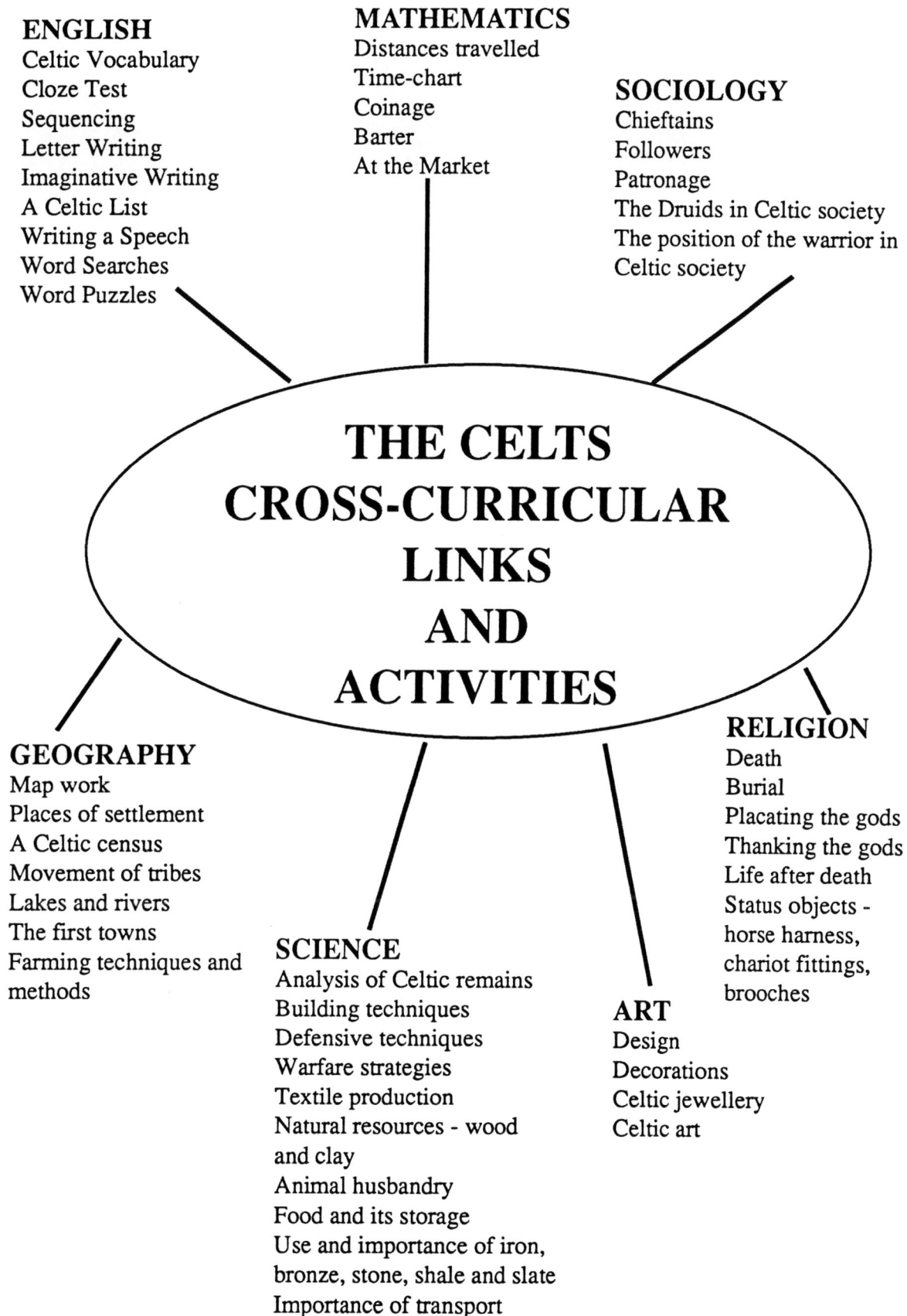

THE CELTS

ENGLISH
Celtic Vocabulary
Cloze Test
Sequencing
Letter Writing
Imaginative Writing
A Celtic List
Writing a Speech
Word Searches
Word Puzzles

MATHEMATICS
Distances travelled
Time-chart
Coinage
Barter
At the Market

SOCIOLOGY
Chieftains
Followers
Patronage
The Druids in Celtic society
The position of the warrior in
Celtic society

THE CELTS CROSS-CURRICULAR LINKS AND ACTIVITIES

GEOGRAPHY
Map work
Places of settlement
A Celtic census
Movement of tribes
Lakes and rivers
The first towns
Farming techniques and
methods

SCIENCE
Analysis of Celtic remains
Building techniques
Defensive techniques
Warfare strategies
Textile production
Natural resources - wood
and clay
Animal husbandry
Food and its storage
Use and importance of iron,
bronze, stone, shale and slate
Importance of transport

ART
Design
Decorations
Celtic jewellery
Celtic art

RELIGION
Death
Burial
Placating the gods
Thanking the gods
Life after death
Status objects -
horse harness,
chariot fittings,
brooches

TEACHERS' NOTES AND RESOURCES

HOW TO USE YOUR MASTER FILE

For many experienced teachers these few lines will seem superfluous. This book is planned to introduce pupils to the history of Britain. The degree of difficulty varies throughout the book. Following the National Curriculum guidelines, it is especially helpful for those between 7 - 11 years but there is much to interest students of all ages. The Celts, Romans, Anglo-Saxons, Vikings and then the Normans* fought and won Britain, bringing their different languages, cultures and customs with them. Two thousand years ago, the Celts inhabited much of western Europe. Fierce, proud and artistic, they were skilled warriors, farmers and metalworkers. They never formed a unified nation but the different Celtic tribes shared a similar way of life. These times influenced the structure of British society and the legacy from this early culture can be seen in the traditions of the six Celtic nations, Brittany, Cornwall, Ireland, Scotland, Wales and the Isle of Man.

1. All the material in this book is photocopiable as defined on page 1. This means that all the material can be used in any way you wish in the classroom situation. Drawings may be photocopied and adapted for further work.

2. Covering sections of the master copies with plain paper enables resource material to be used in different ways.

3. Reduction of the A4 master copies to A5 means that they can be stuck in children's exercise books. The master copies can also be enlarged to A3 to make it easier for students to work on them as a group.

4. Some of your photocopies can be cut up to make additional puzzles and games.

5. It is intended that material be used at different levels depending on the ages and abilities of your pupils.

6. It may be possible to use some of the Teachers' Notes directly with more advanced and brighter students.

7. Some of the worksheets and resources are more difficult than others and we do not envisage any problems with selecting appropriate material.

8. Some of the copy in the teachers' resources may be used in other ways, e.g. as cloze tests, sequencing exercises and so on.

9. Much of the completed work may be used as visual aids around the classroom.

10. Project work may be done individually, in groups and/or with teacher participation.

We hope you enjoy using this book and welcome any comments.

* There are other Master Files on Invaders and Settlers - the Romans, Anglo-Saxons and Vikings.

TEACHERS' NOTES AND RESOURCES

It is important to outline the chronology of events in Great Britain. This may be done with a simple table and drawings.

c100,000 BC The Old Stone Age - man was tribal and nomadic

10,000 BC The Middle Stone Age - man was a hunter living in caves or similar natural shelters

6,000 BC The New Stone Age - man began to grow food and made implements of flint

2,000 BC The Bronze Age

1,200 BC The Celts, the Iron Age

750 BC The Celts settled in Great Britain

They developed farming

400 BC Trade developed with Europe and the Mediterranean

54BC The Romans arrived in Britain

1AD Roman influence expanded: they settled in south-east Britain, Wales and in other areas.

250AD Roman power began to fade. Constantius died at York (306AD)

400 - 600 AD The Age of Saints

787 AD The first Viking raids on Britain

798 AD Danes established at York

1002 AD King Canute reigned (1016 - 35)

He was followed by Edward the Confessor

1066 Norman invasion

The English were defeated by William I at Hastings

It is a good idea to point out that Britain was not united in these times and there was a series of different invaders and settlers. The Celts, the Romans, the Anglo-Saxons, the Picts and Scots, the Vikings and then the Normans were successive waves of peoples who fought for and won Britain. British society was changed and shaped by these invaders and settlers with their different languages, cultures and customs. These early times influenced the structure of British society.

Concentrate on four themes:
1. The Early History of the British Isles.
2. The Invasions and Settlements - including reasons.
3. The Way of Life of the settlers.
4. The Results of the Settlement - the legacy left.

THE CELTS

The Celts were one of these invaders and settlers. The name comes from the word KELTOI used by the Greeks to describe savage tribes living north of the Alps. The arts, social customs and religious beliefs of these people suggest that they had a common cultural heritage.

The Celts were noted for their high spirits and they loved war and excitement. They were hospitable people who enjoyed feasting, drinking and quarrelling. Although regarded as a race they were, in reality, many tribes with a common cultural heritage. To name a few: there were the Belgae, the Canti, the Parisi, the Brigantes, the Iceni, the Dumnonii, the Durotriges and the Prythons (or *Brythons* who gave their name to this country in the word, *Britain*).

They were skilled in making weapons and other goods from iron and the tribes spread from north of the Alps into northern Italy, parts of Yugoslavia, Britain, France, Spain and even into central Europe. The Greeks and Romans came to fear these ferocious warriors in battle and described them as tall, fair and muscular. Militarily, they were almost unstoppable and controlled Europe from the 7th. century BC until they were conquered by the superior organisation and strength of Rome's Legions.

HOW THE CELTS WERE ORGANISED

Explain that there are levels or classes in British society today. For convenience the Celts can also be divided into different levels or groups. It is a good idea to draw a pyramid on the blackboard as you explain the social grouping.

1. the Chieftain,
2. the Druids,
3. the Nobles - the aristocratic and warrior class,
4. Freemen - mostly farmers,
5. Landless men and slaves.

THE CELTS - SOCIAL PYRAMID

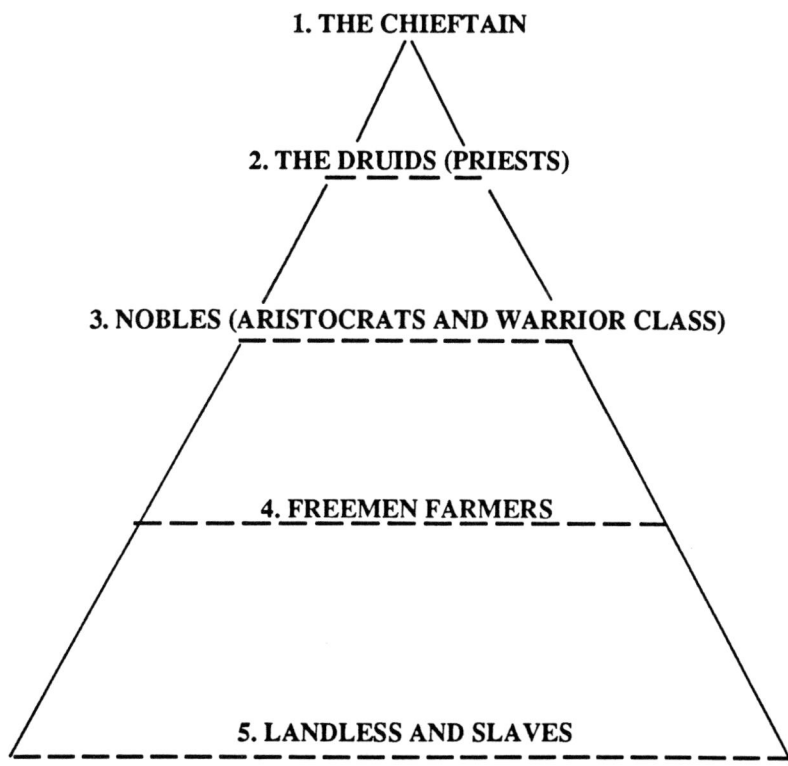

1. THE CHIEFTAIN

2. THE DRUIDS (PRIESTS)

3. NOBLES (ARISTOCRATS AND WARRIOR CLASS)

4. FREEMEN FARMERS

5. LANDLESS AND SLAVES

THE CHIEFTAIN

The King or Chieftain was the head of Celtic society. The senior noble, his status was measured by his success in battle and the number of cattle he owned. He controlled a number of lesser nobles who were responsible for the areas under their command. Most decisions were made by the chieftain but he took advice from the nobles on political and military matters and he consulted the priests or druids on religious matters. The chieftain was expected to be generous and a just ruler in times of peace, and a brave, decisive and successful leader in times of war. Whilst he had rights and duties towards his people, they had rights and duties towards him. [In this way Celtic society was similar to the way Europe was to be organised in later times, that is, the FEUDAL system in which all members of mediaeval society had rights and responsibilities to one another.]

THE DRUIDS

The druids were just below the chieftain in the pecking order. These priests were recruited from families of the nobles but were treated as if they belonged to a higher social class. They were regarded with veneration, respect and a little fear by all classes and carried out magical and religious tasks. They favoured cutting off the heads of captured foes in ritual ceremonies and making sacrifices (including human ones) to please the gods. Druids consulted the omens (happenings or signs which they said predicted what would take place in the future such as the result of a battle) about all sorts of things. They advised the chieftain when it was the best time to go to war and when it was wisest to make peace. They also said that going into combat naked gave warriors magical protection. Druids could recite the tribe's history, religious rituals and the law. Nothing was written down and what they said was not questioned so they had considerable influence and power.

THE NOBLES

They controlled their own areas with the permission of the chieftain. They advised the chieftain, particularly in times of trouble and especially on political and military matters. They led their men into battle and also took part in duels, a noble fighting a champion selected by the enemy in single combat.

FREEMEN FARMERS

Many of the Celts were land-owning farmers and practised mixed farming, that is they raised cattle and grew crops. In some areas, keeping cattle became more important than the cultivation of cereals. The Celts had iron tools which cleared land more easily than the wooden implements of earlier times. They lived in small farms with square fields or in settlements of just a few houses. In Britain, most Celtic houses were circular and surrounded by a timber palisade, a kind of wooden fence, which protected the whole village. In some areas, hilltop towns were constructed. These were forts surrounded by deep ditches, great banks of earth and stone, and walls of wood. In the Celtic world, both farmer and warrior felt insecure and life revolved around attack and defence.

LANDLESS MEN AND SLAVES

In battle, the Celts sometimes took men, women and children prisoner. Often the men were beheaded but some were kept as slaves to be sold and to do the heavy work on the land. Women and children were also used as slaves and worked on the farms. These people were landless, that is they owned nothing.

EVIDENCE ABOUT THE CELTS

It needs to be explained that there is little written evidence about the times of the Celts. The written evidence that does exist comes from Roman writers like Strabo who were not unbiassed. Knowledge of the Celts and early people comes from excavations by archaeologists who dig up remains such as bones, utensils, weapons and pottery. Mention other ways in which historians find out about the past - annual growth rings, aerial photography and radio carbon-dating. Explain the work and importance of an archaeologist. Some remains are found by accident. For example, when the RAF aerodrome in Anglesey was being constructed a whole range of objects was found including a length of iron chain, bits of trumpets and cauldrons and the remains of a war chariot. Some sites such as the Iron Age hillfort of Danebury Ring, six miles southwest of Andover in Hampshire, has been the subject of a planned archaeological dig since 1969. Over half of the 13 acres of the fort have been examined.

INVADERS OR SETTLERS?

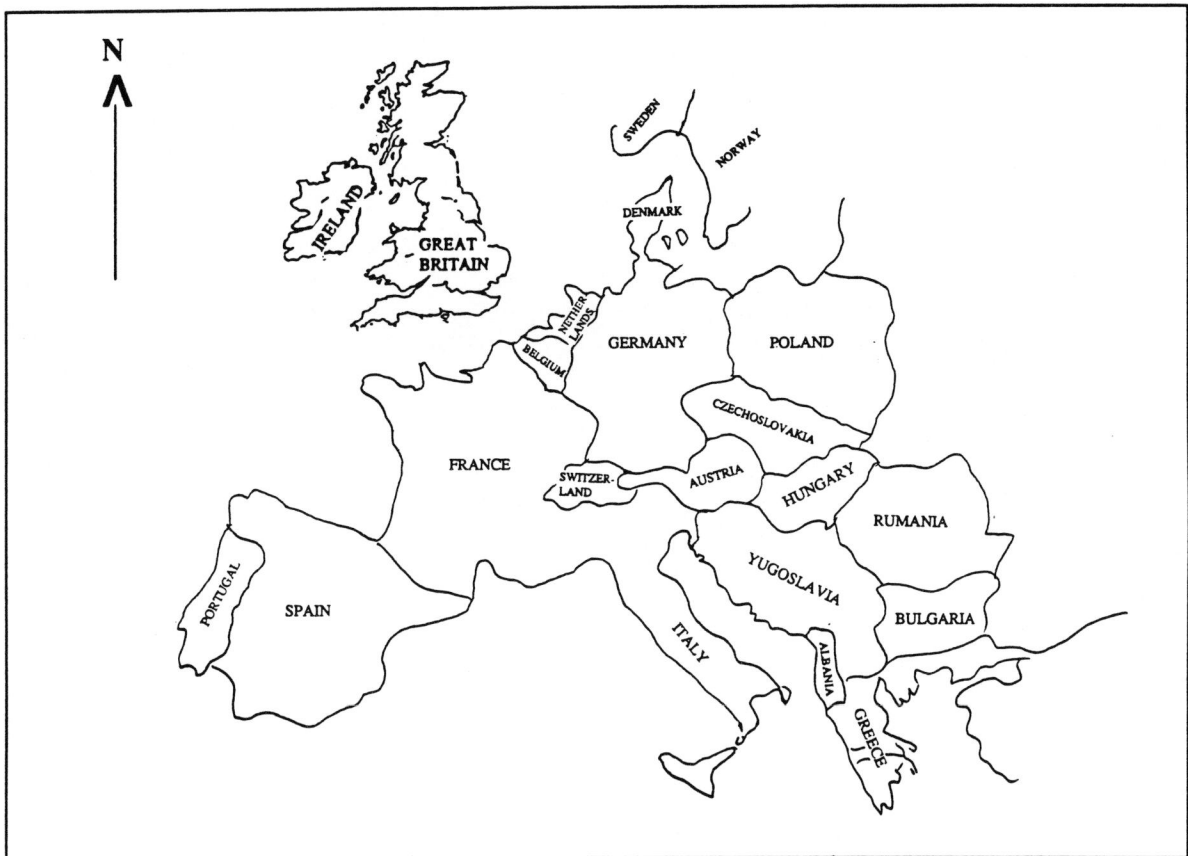

Celtic culture first appeared in Britain between 1000 BC and 500 BC. Tribes first occupied most of Britain south of the Scottish Highlands. The tribes best known to the Romans were the Trinovantes, the Catuvellauni, the Iceni, the Silures, the Ordovices and the Dobunni. Like those in the Bronze Age before them, these peoples built forts with ditches and palisades. Warriors by instinct, the Celts fought not only with their enemies but also raided one another's lands fighting fierce battles with their kinsmen. Combat, often hand to hand and the result of one leader challenging another, usually took place on open ground. Some hillforts, but unfortunately very few, have been the subject of archaeological investigation. Some of the best known include Maiden Castle in Dorset, Danebury Ring in Hampshire, Chanctonbury Ring in Sussex and Castell Henllys in Cardigan, West Wales.

As well as hillforts, there were several other types of settlement. These included **palisaded enclosures** of various sorts, **unenclosed villages, brochs, duns, raths, crannogs** and many more. The **broch** was made of stone and found in Scotland. Some brochs were massive structures: they looked like stone towers and had complex passages and rooms within them. A broch was easily defended. It had no windows and with its thick wooden door the inhabitants could hold out as long as they had supplies. The **dun** was a small, dry-stone walled enclosure usually occupying about half an acre within which dwellings were defended against attack. The **crannog** was a single homestead built on an artificial island at the edge of a lake and is often described as a bog dwelling.

The Celts were essentially **settlers** in Britain and as **permanent** inhabitants were different from the Romans who followed them.

CELTIC LIFE

This is most important and the way of life should be considered in some detail. Essentially, the Celts were settlers rather than invaders. They created permanent sites, living in single farmsteads or small settlements or villages. The economy of the Celts was based on mixed farming. Growing crops and producing grain was the more important but they also reared cattle.

A typical village was surrounded by a palisade as a form of defence against attack. As time went on, the defences became more sophisticated and we shall return to such defences later.

Inside the village was a cluster of circular wooden houses with thatched roofs. These were called round houses and most Iron Age homes were circular. The wooden walls were covered with daub (a mixture of clay, grass and animal dung) to make them weatherproof. In spite of the Celt's instinctive love of fighting, they were settlers rather than invaders. Over most of southern Britain houses were made entirely of timber. Elsewhere, where stone was plentiful, some were made of stone.

Between the houses and off the ground were square-shaped, wooden granaries built on stilts and wooden racks on which hay or fodder was placed to dry in the sun. They also stored food and fodder in underground pits sealed by clay lids. They had ovens for drying and roasting grain. Food and fertilizer were carried in carts.

Inside a roundhouse it was fairly dark. Warmth and light came from the hearth, a fire in the centre (although not every circular building had one). Smoke escaped through the thatched roof. The floor of trodden chalk was swept regularly and skins were used as mats. Furniture was basic with low, wooden tables, stools and wooden platforms covered with skins for beds.

Most wives and children were used to working with their hands and it was not unusual for there to be a vertical loom with a row of heavy weights on a side wall of the roundhouse.

The Celts were skilled ironworkers and their iron tools meant the farmers could work the land better than earlier people. Modern excavators have found axes, billhooks, adzes, saws, sickles, files and harrows all made of iron. For ploughing, the Celts used wooden ards but sometimes these had iron sheaths.

The chief and his family usually lived in a large roundhouse a little apart from the others and with its own palisade. His weapons and body armour for battle would be kept inside while his decorated war chariot drawn by several ponies and their trappings would be kept outside or stabled.

Women were respected in Celtic society and some became tribal leaders. In Britain, one woman ruler Boudicca (Boadicea), Queen of the Iceni tribe in East Anglia, led a revolt against the Romans in AD 61 which was nearly successful.

The Celts' diet was based mainly on cereals such as wheat and barley. The two staple crops were spelt wheat (Triticum spelta) and hulled six-row barley (Hordeum polystichum). Bread was baked in permanent clay-built ovens. The Celts loved porridge and cereals were used not only in bread but in stews. The more aristocratic ate meat : the farmers reared cows, sheep and pigs. Their favourite meat seems to have been pork and choice cuts of roast boar were kept for leaders and heroes. Excavation of graves has shown that joints of pork or even a whole boar were buried with dead warriors to provide the first feast in the underworld.

The Celts loved feasting, eating, drinking, talking, singing and gambling with dice made of bone, often over several days to celebrate victories and to reward warriors for success. A boar would be roasted on a wrought iron spit and food prepared in large cauldrons or stone-built tubs with iron hoops and bronze bindings. The lower classes drank mead and cider and wheaten beer called cornia prepared with honey and beer. The Greeks and Romans were impressed by the amount these warriors could drink. After the feasts and strong drink, they often slept where they fell. Aristocratic Celts drank wine neat, to the disgust of the Romans who diluted their liquor with water.

ATTACK AND DEFENCE

ATTACK

The Greek writer Strabo said of the Celts, *The whole nation . . . is war-mad, both high spirited and ready for battle, but otherwise simple and not uncultured.* He related how a warrior wore a long sword fastened on the right side and a long shield. He also carried the 'madaris', a kind of spear, a wooden weapon to throw at the enemy in battle. Some of the spears were made with a straight head whilst some were twisted with breaks so that the weapon not only cut but also tore the flesh of the enemy.

To protect himself a warrior carried an oval-shaped shield in the left hand which was big enough to cover most of his body. He also wore a helmet probably made of leather and decorated with animals and birds and sometimes with the horn of an animal. Diodorus Siculus says of these helmets,

> *On their heads they wore bronze helmets which possess projecting figures lending the appearance of enormous stature to the warrior. In some cases horns form one piece with the helmet while in other cases it is the relief figures on the fore parts of birds or quadrupeds.*

Warriors were very superstitious. Some fought in the nude believing that this gave them supernatural protection. Many decorated their bodies blue with a vegetable dye, woad, and coated their hair with chalk wash drawing it up into spikes to give them a terrifying appearance.

Celtic warriors also believed that noise could frighten their opponents. They yelled, beat the sides of their carts and wagons and blew war trumpets. *Their trumpets,* wrote Diodorus, *are of a peculiar barbaric kind. They blow into them and produce a harsh sound which suits the tumult of war.* The trumpets, called carnyx, were long and crowned with animals. The Celts were great psychologists, attempting to frighten their opponents into submission before battle started and carrying out all the superstitions needed to have the support of the gods on their side.

Diodorus described the general war preparations, the cavalry and chariots and the overall battle plans with nobles and supporters,

> *They bring . . . as their attendants free men, chosen from among the poorer class, whom they use as charioteers and shield bearers in battle . . . When the armies are drawn up . . . they are wont to advance before the battle-line and to challenge the bravest of their opponents to single combat, at the same time brandishing before them their arms so as to terrify their foe. And when someone accepts their challenge to battle, they loudly recite the deeds of valour of their ancestors and proclaim their own valorous quality, at the same time abusing and making little of their opponent and generally attempting to rob him beforehand of his fighting spirit.*

The historian, Polybius, described the battle between the Celts and the Romans in Tuscany 225 BC:
> The Romans . . . *were terrified by the fire order of the Celtic host and the dreadful din, for there were innumerable horn blowers and trumpeters, and the whole army was shouting their war cries at the same time: there was such a tumult of sound that it seemed that . . . all the country round had got a voice and caught up the cry. Very terrifying too were the appearance and gestures of all the naked warriors in front, all in the prime of life and finely built men, and all in the leading companies richly adorned with gold torques and armlets.*

The Celts believed that the head contained the soul, the centre of the emotions and life itself. It was their custom to cut off the heads of their enemies and to ride home with them strapped on the necks of their horses. The heads were then displayed in the tribal home for strangers to admire. The more important the enemy, the greater the value of the head and the heads of the most distinguished enemies were preserved.

DEFENCE

Many Celts lived in specially designed hillforts. Excavations have shown a series of defences built at different phases in their development. Elementary defences were wooden palisades. These were vertical walls of timber to keep out attackers. Often such defences were abandoned for a steep, sloping glacis, most difficult to attack. Many forts had a number of gates. At Danebury, for example, an outer gate was defended from earthworks and a command post. If the enemy succeeded in getting through this, there was another barrier, an inner gate. Between the gates was a treacherous, twisting road, flanked by high flint-built walls. The defenders could fire at invaders at will from the sides of this route and the inner gate had a fighting platform on top manned by defenders. One of the most common weapons used in the defence of a fort was the sling. Entrance to a fort was constructed so that the two gates were always in sight and in range of the defenders. All parts of the defensive structure could be protected by expert slingers.

RELIGION

The druids were the priests of the Celts, the wise men of their society. They were healers, teachers, musicians, poets and judges. Nothing was written down, Celtic was not a written language and so they were responsible for the care of all knowledge and for passing it on. Amongst the things they had to remember were ritual procedures, magic formulae, prayers, medical knowledge, folk history, law and genealogies.Caesar describes their duties as, *they officiate at the worship of the gods, regulate public and private sacrifices and give rulings on all religious questions* . . . Druids were exempt from taxes and military service and had to memorise all the teachings of the tribes.

At the core of their teachings was the belief that the soul did not die but passed into another body. Because of this, the Celts had little fear of death and had a strong belief in an afterlife. Neither did they believe in sin or punishment.

One of the rituals practised by the druids is described by Pliny. He tells that mistletoe, well known for its healing properties, was considered to be particularly potent if found growing near an oak tree and cut in a special way. First, two white bulls were brought to the place. Then a white-robed druid cut the mistletoe with a golden sickle and the branch was caught in a white robe by those below. The bulls were then sacrificed while prayers were said to the god. It was believed that mistletoe cut in this way and taken in a drink could make barren animals fertile and was an antidote for all poisons.

It has been established from archaeological evidence that the Celts worshipped more than 400 different gods. There was no one god common to all the peoples and it is possible that every Celtic family had its own god whilst believing in the existence of hundreds of others. As far as the Celts were concerned, the supernatural was everywhere. The spirits were in trees, mountains and rivers, strangely shaped rocks and in marshes and bogs. Gods were responsible for the weather and the seasons and they controlled the natural world of which men were a part. If there was a disaster such as famine or disease, it happened because the gods were angry and had to be placated or appeased. A sacrifice or offering was needed to make the gods look on the people more favourably.

Some animals such as bulls, boars, dogs and birds were sacred to the Celts. They may not have believed these animals were gods, but the creatures were used in religious rituals.

The trinity was an important idea and often their gods were represented with three heads (tricephalos). The idea of the *Three Mothers* appears in nearly all parts of the Celtic world and occasionally the sacred bull appears with three horns instead of the usual two.

Horned gods were common. Cernunnos was one of these and was depicted in human form with the horned head of a deer. The main gods were undoubtedly the earth mother-goddess and the tribal father god. The great male god, the god on whom all tribal gods were based, was Dugdá. Translated this means *the god good at everything*. His female counterpart was the Mórrigan described as *the great queen, the mother goddess and the goddess of fertility*. The relationship between these gods explained everything, good and evil, bravery and fear, life and death.

Amongst the important individual gods were

Lug or Lugh, probably a fertility god,
Epona, a horse goddess,
Matres or Matronae, mother goddesses and
Sulis, a female god endowed with powers of healing the sick.

Many references to religion do not deal with gods at all but with the importance of places that were special to the Celts. These were their sanctuaries, sacred woods, sacred lakes, sacred bogs and swamps being the most important. They worshipped their gods not in temples but in these sacred places. There were many such places including a wood near Marseilles, the source of the rivers Marne and Seine. It was at these sanctuaries that vows were taken and sacrifices made. At the mouth of the Seine, for example, excavations have revealed about 190 pieces of wood carvings with more than 20 complete statues dating from the middle of the 1st. century AD. A great hoard was discovered at Llyn Cerrig Bach in Anglesey, North Wales in 1943. It consisted of many weapons, chariot furniture, slave chains with collars attached, cauldrons and fragments of bronze. The find is believed to consist of sacrificial offerings made between the mid 2nd. century BC to the middle of the 1st. century AD.

Animal and human sacrifices were made at these sites too. Criminals were preferred as sacrifices but if there were not enough, other humans were used to make up the numbers. The Romans exaggerated the extent of such sacrifices. Caesar asserts in a typical piece of Roman propaganda, *Some tribes have colossal images made of wickerwork, the limbs of which they fill with living men: they are then set on fire, and the victims are burnt to death*. There is no doubt that human sacrifices were performed and were of considerable ritual importance. It has been argued that such human sacrifices were practised *more commonly at times of communal danger or stress, rather than as part of regular ritual observance*.

In some parts of the world, the Celts dug deep shafts and it has been suggested that they were trying to reach the underworld.

CUSTOMS AND SUPERSTITIONS

Information about Celtic customs comes from ancient writings, archaeological excavations and objects they made which have been found and examined.

SACRIFICES

Sometimes the bodies of people and objects used for sacrifices to please the gods do not decay but are preserved in the soil or wherever they lie. When these remains are examined by experts, archaeologists and historians, they give valuable information about Celtic customs and beliefs. The Celts often threw victims and prized objects into lakes, bogs and rivers to please their gods. Thus, a neck ring and a boat both made of gold were part of a number of such objects found at Broighter in north-west Ireland. A series of objects was also found in a marsh near the lake at Llyn Cerrig Bach on the Isle of Môna now called Anglesey.

Similarly, the corpse of an Iron Age man was found in a peat bog at Tollund in the Jutland area of Denmark. Discovered in 1950 the man had been put to death probably as a fertility sacrifice to the Goddess of the Earth. Strangled with a leather thong, 'Tollund Man 'was not alone and other bodies, both male and female, were found in the same area. They had been put to death by various methods including hanging, by having their throats cut, by being drowned or buried alive.

SYMBOLS

The Celts believed that some objects such as a torc or ceremonial necklace or neck ring gave them power and protected them from danger. [Today, a crown is seen as a symbol of authority or power and officals such as mayors sometimes wear 'chains of office' around their necks. People also keep charms to bring them luck.]

GODS AND GODDESSES

The Celts believed in many gods and goddesses and that these controlled everything from the weather, a good or bad harvest and fertility to success in battle. They believed that these gods could change shape and take the form of anything in the natural world. They were often thought to be half-animal or half-human, for example, Cernunnos, the horned god. The Celts also believed in the importance of three (the trinity) and some gods were believed to have three heads.

WARRIORS

These men had armour, helmet and shields and went into battle well equipped. Some warriors were used as shock troops - they stripped naked before going into battle believing their nudity would terrify their enemies and give them supernatural powers. Some smeared their blonde hair with chalk-wash to make it look brighter and drew it up into spikes to make their appearance more awesome.

FOES

Celts believed that the head contained the soul and cut off the heads of their enemies. Skulls were kept in pots (in cedar oil), put on poles and (in France in one case) incorporated into a temple doorway.

RITUAL MASSACRES

The Romans declared that the Celts took part in ritual killings. This was probably propaganda and there is no evidence that such massacres were widespread. However, human sacrifices did occur, carried out by Druids (magicians or priests) in ceremonies to please the gods. The Druids decided when these should take place and where, usually in dark groves which they claimed were sacred.

OAK TREE GROVES

These were favourite places for ceremonies, especially religious ones with people and animals being used. Some plants were believed to have magical powers. Mistletoe was thought to have such powers and people chosen to undergo torture or sacrifice were given mistletoe berries before their ordeal to dull their senses.

SPRINGS

The Celts found spring water fascinating. It often contained substances which had healing properties and the Celts

looked on springs and rivers as female gods. They offered wooden carvings of the diseased part of a person's body to these goddesses hoping for a cure. Carvings of eyes, hands, heads, legs and internal organs have been found in springs and at the source of rivers.

GRAVES AND BURIALS

Recent excavations have shown that excarnation may have been used as a method of burial, that is the dead body was exposed to the elements possibly on a raised dais or platform until the spirit finally departed. After that the remains may have been dealt with in a number of ways. The Celts believed in ritual burials and buried things used by the dead in life or likely to be needed by the deceased in the afterlife. Some burials examined have contained a four-wheeled wagon on which the dead person was placed. One of the most important finds was a tomb at Vix, Châtillon-sur-Seine, France, discovered in 1953. This burial chamber contained the skeleton of a woman who died when she was about 30 and was surrounded by jewellery, bracelets, torques, brooches, a necklace and a golden diadem which had been buried with her.

FESTIVALS

The calendar was regulated by the druids and calculated using the movement of the moon. Time was measured by the number of nights that passed and the times of festivals could be fixed in the year. Such festivals were celebrated by eating and drinking to excess. Greek writers record that the Celts sat on the floor on skins or dried grass and the food was placed on low, wooden tables. There were four major festivals in the Celtic calendar, the Samain, Imbolc, Beltine and Lughnasa.

SAMAIN OR SAMHAIN (31st October to 1st November)

This was the beginning of the Celtic year. It was the festival of the dead when the barriers between man and the supernatural were believed to disappear and people from the spirit world could be seen by people on earth. It was believed to be a time of great danger. (Modern equivalent: All Souls'/All Saints'/Martinmas.)

IMBOLC (1st. February)

This was the time of fertility and fruitfulness, the time, for example, when lambs are born. (Modern equivalent St Brigid's/Candlemas.)

BELTINE (BELTANE or BELTAINE) (1st. May)

This was the festival of hope and optimism celebrated with feasting and sacrifices to the gods. Fires were lit and cattle driven between them as a purification rite. It was a time of rejoicing by people thankful to have survived the winter, a time to celebrate the fertility of crops and the birth of young animals. (Modern equivalent might be Whitsun.)

LUGHNASA (LUGNASADH) (1st. August)

Festival of the god Lugh. This celebrated a successful harvest and the rearing of stock. (Modern equivalent Lammas/ Harvest festival.)

ART, CLOTHES AND JEWELLERY

Artistically, the Celts were very talented and they loved to make beautiful things. By the 7th. century BC, they had learnt all the skills needed to work bronze and knew how to extract copper and tin. They had also learnt to extract and forge iron, and had mastered the techniques of using graphite and haematite to decorate pottery. They were also able to use materials like gold, silver, coral, amber and glass to make luxury objects. One writer records that in short, *the surviving material remains of Celtic culture show that society was endowed with technology and the craft skills unsurpassed in Europe until the eighteenth century AD.*

ART

One of the most important features was that they used their art on everyday objects, they united the beautiful and the practical. There are a series of styles.

1. From the end of the Bronze Age to the Hallstatt period.
2. The La Tène period.
3. Post La Tène period - Britain.
4. Irish period.

The following are some of the treasures found in various parts of the world.

The Basse-Yutz Flagons
These are a pair of bronze wine flagons dating from the 4th. century BC. Found at Moselle in eastern France, they are decorated with a number of animals with ducks on the spout.

The Gundestrup Cauldron
This is a silver-plated bronze cauldron measuring 27 inches (68 cm) across. Discovered at Gundestrup in Denmark in 1891, it is richly decorated on the outside with carvings of different gods and on the inside with scenes from Celtic mythology.

The Desborough Mirror
From the 1st. century BC until 43 AD the Celts made a variety of bronze mirrors with elaborate handles and engravings on their backs. This mirror was discovered at Desborough in Northamptonshire in 1908. It was made in the 1st. century AD.

The Witham Shield
This was found in the River Witham near Lincoln and has embossed Celtic patterns and fine engraving. The figure of a boar was part of the earlier decoration but this has now disappeared.

The Battersea Horned Helmet
The bronze horned helmet and bronze shield found in the Thames at Battersea are two further examples of Celtic workmanship.

CLOTHES

The Celts were concerned about their personal appearance. Very few were fat which was socially unacceptable and women used mirrors, make-up and tweezers to pluck their eyebrows. Unfortunately, very little is known about the clothes worn by the Celts because few have survived. A chieftain would have worn a tunic, plaid trousers and cloak. These were brightly coloured and it is possible that Scottish tartans continue this tradition. Leather belts were popular from earliest times and brooches (fibulae) were used to fasten cloaks at the breast or on the shoulder. Such a chief

One of the Basse-Yutz Flagons

The Desborough Mirror

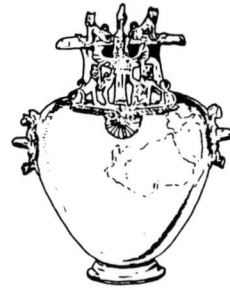

A Bronze Hydria

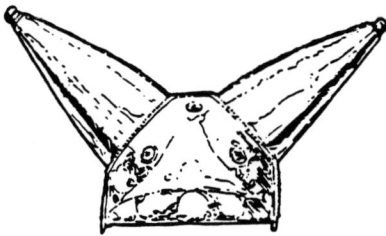

The Battersea Horned Helmet

The Gundestrup Cauldron

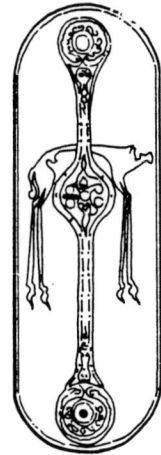

The Witham Shield

Celtic women wore long dresses down to their ankles. Their skirts were gathered in the middle and held up by leather belts to which a number of ornaments might be attached. There were no buttons and clothes were fastened by different types of pins and brooches.

Colour these pictures using crayons or felt tipped pens.

Drawings not to scale.

would also have worn a sword or dagger, a torc around his neck and gold bracelets or arm rings. In battle a chief would probably have worn a bronze helmet with a tall crest giving him extra height. In this way the Celts towered over their enemy in battle giving them a psychological advantage. One Greek traveller wrote *They use amazing colours, brightly dyed shirts with flowing patterns and trousers called breeches ...* and *Their nobles let their moustaches grow so long that they hide their mouths and, when they eat, get entangled in their food ...*

Men wore a loose tunic and plaid trousers and were fond of bright colours and patterned cloth. The women wore long dresses down to their ankles. Their skirts were gathered in the middle and held up by leather belts to which a number of ornaments might be attached. There were no buttons and clothes were fastened by different types of pins and brooches.

Dio Cassius described Boudicca (Boadicea), the Queen of the Iceni thus: *She was huge of frame, terrifying of aspect and with a harsh voice. A great mass of bright red hair fell to her knees: she wore a great twisted golden torc, and a tunic of many colours, over which was a thick mantle, fastened by a brooch. Now she grasped a spear, to strike fear into all who watched her.*

JEWELLERY

Celtic men and women loved to wear jewellery. Numerous ornamental pins and brooches have been found by archaeologists. These were often decorated with human and animal faces. Also torcs worked in brass, silver or gold and with their ends formed into human heads and lion masks have been discovered. Gold bracelets or arm bands were popular among the nobility and fine metalwork including coloured enamel highlights was used in many of the pieces. Sunflower pins were also worn - these had carefully crafted heads which shone brightly on the wearer's clothes.

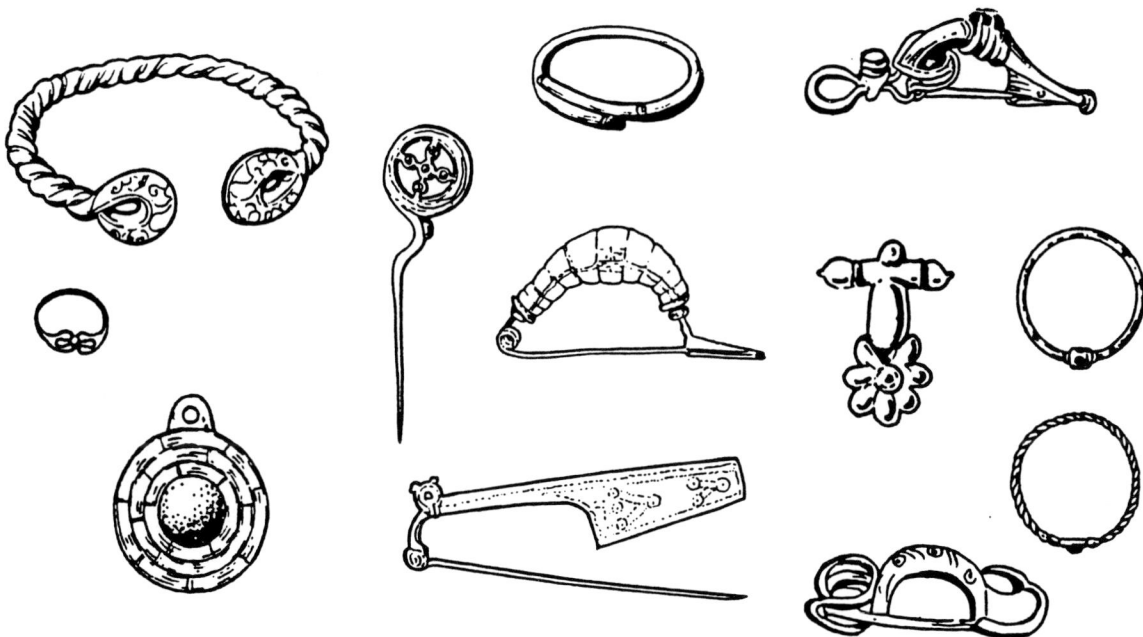

Celtic jewellery (not to scale).

THE 'HEROIC' AGE

In 1858 an important discovery was made at La Tène, on the banks of Lake Neuchatel in Switzerland. There, large quantities of Iron Age metalwork were found including swords, spears, shields, horse gear, tools of all kinds, jewellery, ornaments, coins and many other objects. At first, it was thought that these items were thrown into the lake to appease the gods but later research suggests that the site was probably a domestic and industrial settlement on dry land which was suddenly flooded. The La Tène culture which began about 600 BC was regarded as the finest period of Celtic domination, their *heroic age*. They expanded into the Balkans, Greece and Asia Minor, they sacked Rome about 390 BC and Delphi around 279 BC. Before the La Tène culture was over, the Celts had penetrated into Britain and Ireland.

Artistically too, La Tène culture contributed to luxury items in weapons and jewellery such as many brooches decorated with human and animal heads. Later, in the second half of the 4th. century, enamel, first in red and then in other colours, was added to the bronze work. Ducks and birds were included in pottery items and in Britain bronze mirrors were made with patterns cut into their surfaces.

THE CELTIC ECLIPSE

From about 150 BC the influence of the Roman Empire spread throughout Europe. By 120 BC, southern France had been annexed and a little later Gaul (modern France and Belgium) had been conquered. Soon after 100 BC changes occurred in Britain too, mainly as a result of the coming of the Romans. In 55 and 54 BC, Julius Caesar invaded Britain and from AD 43, Roman legions landed and began their permanent conquest of these islands. The Celts began to depend less on their hillforts and many fell into disuse. Burial rites changed and there were developments in technology. Britain was no longer isolated from the continent and became accustomed to new imports and ideas from Europe and the Mediterranean. New settlements emerged especially on important roads and river crossings. These were Britain's first towns. Many like Calleva (Silchester) and Londinium (London) became tribal capitals while others became established provincial capitals. At these places regular markets met and coins were minted replacing the old system of barter and making it easier to trade.

THE CELTIC LEGACY

In some parts of the world especially in the Highlands and Islands of Scotland, Ireland, the Isle of Man, Wales, Cornwall and Britanny, Celtic culture lives on. These peoples are proud of their heritage and such traditions remain influential. Folk customs have been carefully preserved with 'modern' culture imposed on them. In Wales, for example, the Eisteddfod was revived in 1789 and has continued ever since: the contestants and audiences are never allowed to forget their Celtic ancestry. In Scotland, there are the Highland Games, gatherings featuring contests of skill and strength such as tossing the caber, throwing the hammer, folk dancing and playing the bagpipes. In the Highlands and Islands, the clan system is important and relates back to the Celtic social system.

The traditions remain also in the languages spoken. Irish Gaelic is taught in all Ireland's schools and is spoken by just over a million people although in areas other than those of the north and west it is still very much a second language. Scottish Gaelic was the everyday language of Scotland until the late 17th century when English became the language of education and government. It has enjoyed a revival in recent years and is spoken by some 69,000 Scots. Breton, spoken by the people of Brittany, is quite close to Welsh. Over 300,000 speak the language but unfortunately most of the speakers are aged and the language could decline quickly. In the Isle of Man, Manx is spoken for ceremonial occasions like the meetings of Tynwald and attempts are being made to revive the language for more everyday use. In Cornwall, the language is all but dead although there are some signs of an academic revival. In Wales, over half a million speak Welsh especially in the north and west of the Principality. Welsh has been given equal status with English and is used extensively in street and road signs, and in official documents which are printed in both languages. Wales has a TV and a radio station devoted to its own language and Welsh was saved from extinction in the south partly by the policy of providing bilingual schools in the area. The National Curriculum states that all children should have instruction in the Welsh language.

In all the Celtic lands, evidence of earlier times remain in street, road and place names. *Ewenny* in Glamorgan, for example, comes from *Aventia*, the name of a Celtic goddess, *Denbigh* in Clwyd is derived from the Celtic *dounon* meaning an enclosed safe place; *Clarach* in Dyfed has the Celtic suffix *-ach* meaning water and *claer* meaning *bright and clear*. Individual names throughout the 'Celtic fringe' also have ancient origins. Celtic Christian names survive in names like Brian, Donald, Emlyn, Deirdre, Morwenna and Muriel.

VISITING HISTORICAL SITES

THE IMPORTANCE OF VISITS

A visit to a Celtic site or a museum brings the threads of the study together. 'Chalk and talk' are now turned into reality and pupils can see for themselves how the Celts lived and worked. Observation is the keynote but there may be possibilities of participation in the Celtic way of life and of role play. Fortunately, throughout Britain there are many Iron Age sites(especially forts) and excellent museum displays. Try to visit the chosen site alone before taking a group or class.

PREPARATION FOR A SITE VISIT

BEFORE THE VISIT
Choose a site that is appropriate and can be easily reached. The nearer this is to the school the better. Make a list of the reasons for and the aims of the visit. Decide which National Curriculum topics are to be covered and which attainment targets you wish to meet. If possible visit the site yourself before you take the class. Most sites have an educational officer - make contact and discuss your visit with him/her. Also most sites have teachers' notes and worksheets which are usually helpful and save a great deat of time. You may wish to modify them to suit your class and your own objectives. It is very important to prepare the children for the visit. The site will seem exciting and strange to them when they arrive. They may wander off aimlessly, waste time and possibly get into dangerous situations.

Decide what you are going to tell the children about the site before the visit. Few are likely to be born archaeologists or natural historians and they need enough information to enable them to understand what they will see during the visit. Slides, photographs, ground/site plans are helpful beforehand if they are available. It may be useful to talk about Celtic sites in general and then discuss the site you are planning to visit in particular. One visit is not going to cover everything and so decide exactly what you want to concentrate on. Depending on the age and abilities of the chidlren, keep it short and keep it simple. Above all, they should enjoy it educationally and socially.

It may be necessary to enhance the children's visual skills. The visit may involve using the following skills at some level.

1. Observation skills.
2. Recording skills.
3. Being able to make comparisons.
4. Being able to make deductions.
5. Reading, writing and comprehension skills.
6. Measuring skills.
7. Estimating skills.

8. The ability to read maps.
9. The ability to read plans.
10. Mathematical skills.
11. Scientific skills.
12. Social skills, especially sharing and communicating.

A sense of time may be learned from the visit and youngsters may realise the importance of historical evidence. Aesthetically, the group may gain a great deal from what they see. Pupils need guidance about what to do with the information and data they collect at the site. This is mainly a question of organising the material. Practise for this by organising a survey before the visit. This could be a survey of the school, the school grounds, a village or an area of your local town. This should be simple but it is helpful to observe a familiar place closely and discover the relationship between information on a flat piece of paper like a map or diagram drawn by the pupil and the 3D environment.

Devise your own activity pack for use on the site. This should include illustrations, a questionnaire and questions requiring observation and deduction.

TEACHERS' CHECK LIST

On your personal visit before taking your group or class consider the following.

1. Geography of the land. Consider this, the lie of the land and the geology of the site.

2. Location of the site. Why was the site chosen? Was it mainly for military purposes? Did it start as a camp and how did it develop? Is it near water resources, a river crossing, or did it become part of a trade route? Did it develop into an important settlement or town?

3. Was the site occupied before Celtic times? Is there any evidence of prehistoric man? If so, how did the Celts change it?

4. Defence. Would the site have been easy to defend? Is there any evidence left of defensive structures? Were there multiple points of defence? Is the location ideal for withstanding an attack? Were there any defensive disadvantages? Was the site ever attacked? If so, what was the result?

5. Attack. Is it a suitable site from which to wage war? What elements of cover are there for an attacking force? Is the site easy to withdraw to after attacking the enemy?

6. Weapons. What has been discovered at the site? What else was probably used?

7. Discoveries. Have there been any important discoveries or finds at the site? If so, be prepared to pinpoint them so that you can discuss them with the children.

8. Reconstructions. Have there been any reconstructions at the site (e.g. the building of a Celtic roundhouse). If so, be prepared to discuss them with the children.

9. When was the settlement used? Approximate dates are useful. Decide whether it was used in peace or war or both?

10. Buildings/Dwellings. Consider these. What kinds of homes were they, what makes them distinctly Celtic, what was their size and location? Were there any special structures, e.g. a chief's dwelling?

11. Size of the community. Consider the size and social structure of the community. Were there any specialists such as potters, craftsmen, farmers, priests? What evidence is there of slaves and their tasks?

12. Food. What evidence is there about diet, cooking and cooking utensils? What can be learned about the storage and preparation of food? Is there any evidence of the grinding of flour, e.g. a quern?

13. Meat. Is there any evidence of food processing, meat eating or meat cooking, e.g. fire dogs, ovens or cooking pots?

14. Food preservation. Are there any details of the storage of grain? Was food preserved?

15. Natural resources. What were the natural resources of the site - such as wood, stone, clay or charcoal? Were there any natural resources close by? Were there any others? Have these been exhausted?

16. Skilled work. Is there any evidence of skilled work such as making cloth, leather goods, iron goods, weapons, pots and decorative pottery, jewellery ... ?

17. Metal working. Is there any evidence of metal working (iron, lead, tin, bronze, iron, silver, gold) at the site? Look for equipment, tools, jewellery and artefacts. Is there any evidence of Celtic coins being produced?

18. Other materials. Is there any evidence of the use of stone, shale, slate or other materials on the site? (If so have they been used practically or aesthetically or both?)

19. Clothes. Is there any evidence of the production of woollen or linen material and clothes?

20. Finds of special interest. Have there been any finds of special interest such as those which conferred status or position - torques, shields, swords, helmets, brooches and other jewellery?

20. Religion. Is there any evidence of religious worship or ceremonies? What gods were worshipped?

22. Burials. Is there any evidence of death and burial ceremonies on the site? Were articles buried with the dead? What evidence is there of Celtic superstitions?

23. Celtic properties. Is there evidence of items or buildings that are particularly associated with the Celts - torques, druid stones and so on?

24. Decline. How did the site decline? What came after? How is the site looked after today?

25. Excavations. Has the site been fully excavated? What work remains to be done?

SOME SITES TO VISIT

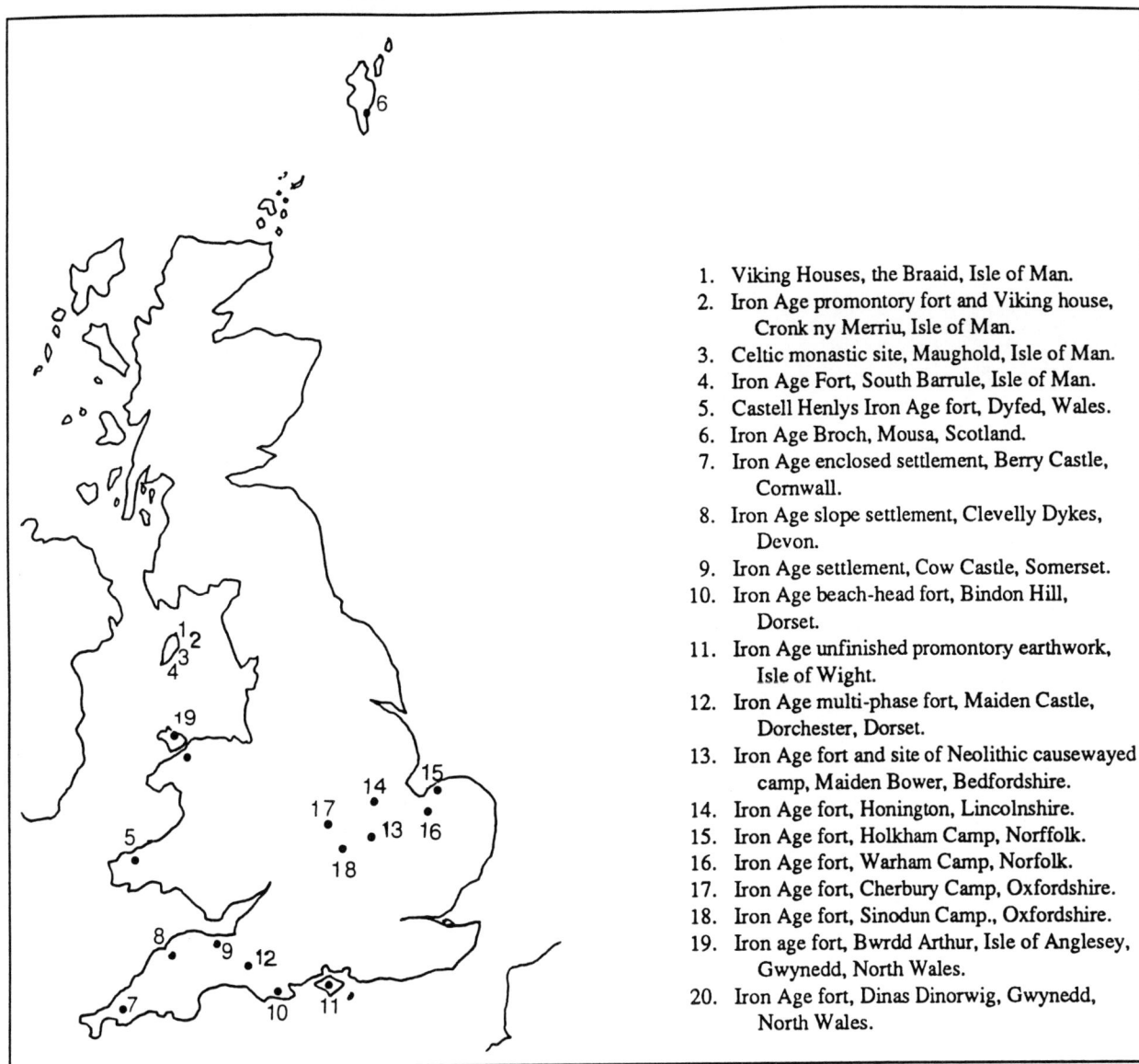

1. Viking Houses, the Braaid, Isle of Man.
2. Iron Age promontory fort and Viking house, Cronk ny Merriu, Isle of Man.
3. Celtic monastic site, Maughold, Isle of Man.
4. Iron Age Fort, South Barrule, Isle of Man.
5. Castell Henlys Iron Age fort, Dyfed, Wales.
6. Iron Age Broch, Mousa, Scotland.
7. Iron Age enclosed settlement, Berry Castle, Cornwall.
8. Iron Age slope settlement, Clevelly Dykes, Devon.
9. Iron Age settlement, Cow Castle, Somerset.
10. Iron Age beach-head fort, Bindon Hill, Dorset.
11. Iron Age unfinished promontory earthwork, Isle of Wight.
12. Iron Age multi-phase fort, Maiden Castle, Dorchester, Dorset.
13. Iron Age fort and site of Neolithic causewayed camp, Maiden Bower, Bedfordshire.
14. Iron Age fort, Honington, Lincolnshire.
15. Iron Age fort, Holkham Camp, Norffolk.
16. Iron Age fort, Warham Camp, Norfolk.
17. Iron Age fort, Cherbury Camp, Oxfordshire.
18. Iron Age fort, Sinodun Camp., Oxfordshire.
19. Iron age fort, Bwrdd Arthur, Isle of Anglesey, Gwynedd, North Wales.
20. Iron Age fort, Dinas Dinorwig, Gwynedd, North Wales.

The map indicates twenty Iron Age sites. Teachers are advised that a comprehensive map of Celtic sites in Britain, 'Ancient Britain' is published by the Ordnance Survey. This map is certainly worth getting and will show the sites nearest to your school.

AT THE SITE

Make use of the surroundings of the site as well as buildings there. Let the pupils study these surroundings including flora, fauna, trees (include bark rubbings if appropriate), animal habitats and so on. Instead of or as well as the guidance from activity sheets, the children may be asked to solve a problem from the past. Examples are:

You are the chief in charge of a Celtic hill fort. Say how you would prepare to repel an enemy attack.

You are leaving a Celtic fort. Say what people you would leave behind and why.

Show how this Celtic settlement was organised in times of peace.

A group of foreign tourists who have no previous knowledge of the Celts are going to visit the site. List the main things you would want them to know. Why have you chosen these?

The children may imagine they are Celts living at the site. Give them roles to play and work out how these roles may be fulfilled. If it is practical, pupils can dress up as Celts and enact an event from history such as the revolt of Boudicca or the capture of Caractacus. The use of an unfamiliar site in this way may be difficult and not as useful as using role play as part of the follow up.

FOLLOW UP TO A VISIT

To reinforce the visit you might consider the following when you return to the classroom.

1. Devise a quiz to find out how much the children have learned.
2. Devise other written work especially making them see the site as a place where people lived and worked. How did the site operate on a daily basis? Use actual characters from Celtic history if possible.
3. Guide the children to write reports on particular aspects of the site - the location, the chief's dwelling, a Celtic roundhouse.
4. Use the activity pack/worksheets/guide book.
5. Organise the pupils to make a display of any written work - drawings, maps, ground plans, photographs ... Develop this for use in the classroom and classify and label any objects. Some children may make models (some accurately scaled) costumed figures and measured drawings.
6. Pinpoint any technology from the site, e.g. earthworks. Spinning, dyeing, weaving making weapons or pots are part of this.
7. Pinpoint the diet and ways in which food was cooked.
8. Pupils could make a frieze or collage. Brass or other rubbings may be possible.
9. The pupils could write and act a play or situation which might have occurred on the site such as a conversation between a Celtic warrior and a boy listening to tales of his exploits.
10. Use slides, drawings, photographs and so on to prepare an audio-visual presentation. Tape-slide sequences. Presentations or a video presentation may be possible depending on the site and the age and abilities of the children.
11. Pupils may examine drawings or photographs from the site. They could ask themselves why these materials are important and what they are meant to convey.

Finally it is necessary to evaluate the visit objectively and write a brief report on how such a visit may be improved next time.

BOOKLIST

Some useful titles:

Aylett, J. F. *In Search of History, Early Times to 1066*, Edward Arnold.
Brailsford, J. *Early Celtic Masterpieces from Britain*, British Museum Publications.
Brown, P. *The Book of Kells*, Thames and Hudson.
Chadwick, N. *The Celts*, Penguin.
Childe, V. Gn. *The Dawn of European Civilisation*, Routledge and Kegan Paul.
Chippendale, C. *Stonehenge Complete*, Thames and Hudson.
Collis, J. *European Iron Age*, Batsford.
Cunliffe, B. *The Celtic World*, The Bodley Head.
Delaney, F. *The Celts*, Harper Collins.
Dillon, M. and Chadwick, N. *The Celtic Realms*, Thames and Hudson.
Filip, J. *Celtic Civilisation and its Heritage*, Collett.
Fox, C. *A Find of the Early Iron Age from Llyn Cerrig Bach*, Anglesey. National Museum of Wales.
Fox, C. *The Personality of Britain*, National Museum of Wales.
Guest, C. (ed.) *The Mabinogion*, Folio Society.
Humphreys, E. *The Taliesin Tradition*, The Bodley Head.
Jackson, K. H. *A Celtic Miscellany*, Routledge and Kegan Paul.
Kilbride-Jones, H.E. *Celtic Craftsmanship in Bronze*, Croom Helm.
Kruta, V. and Forman, W. *The Celts of the West*, Orbis.
Laing, L. *The Archaeology of Late Celtic Britain and Scotland*, Methuen.
Laing, L. *Celtic Britain*, Routledge and Kegan Paul.
McCana, P. *Celtic Mythology*, Newnes Books.
MacGregor, *Early Celtic Art in North Britain*, Leicester University Press.
MacNeil, M. The Festival of Lughnasa, OUP.
Norton-Taylor, D. *The Celts*, Time-Life Books.
Norton-Taylor, D. *The Celts*, Thames and Hudson.
Piggott, S. *Ancient Europe*, Edinburgh University Press.
Piggot, S. *The Druids*, Thames and Hudson.
Powell, T.G.E. *The Celts*, Thames and Hudson.
Ross, A. *Everday Life of the Pagan Celts*, Batsford.
Rhys, J. *Celtic Folklore, Welsh and Manx*, OUP.
Sharkey, J. *Celtic Mysteries - the Ancient Religion*, Crossroads Publishing.
Stead, T.M. *The Battersea Shield*, British Museum Publications.
Wheeler, R.E.M. *Maiden Castle, Dorset*, Reports of the Research Committee of the Society of Antiquaries of London.

PUPILS' RESOURCES - WORKSHEETS

COUNTRIES CELTS INVADED

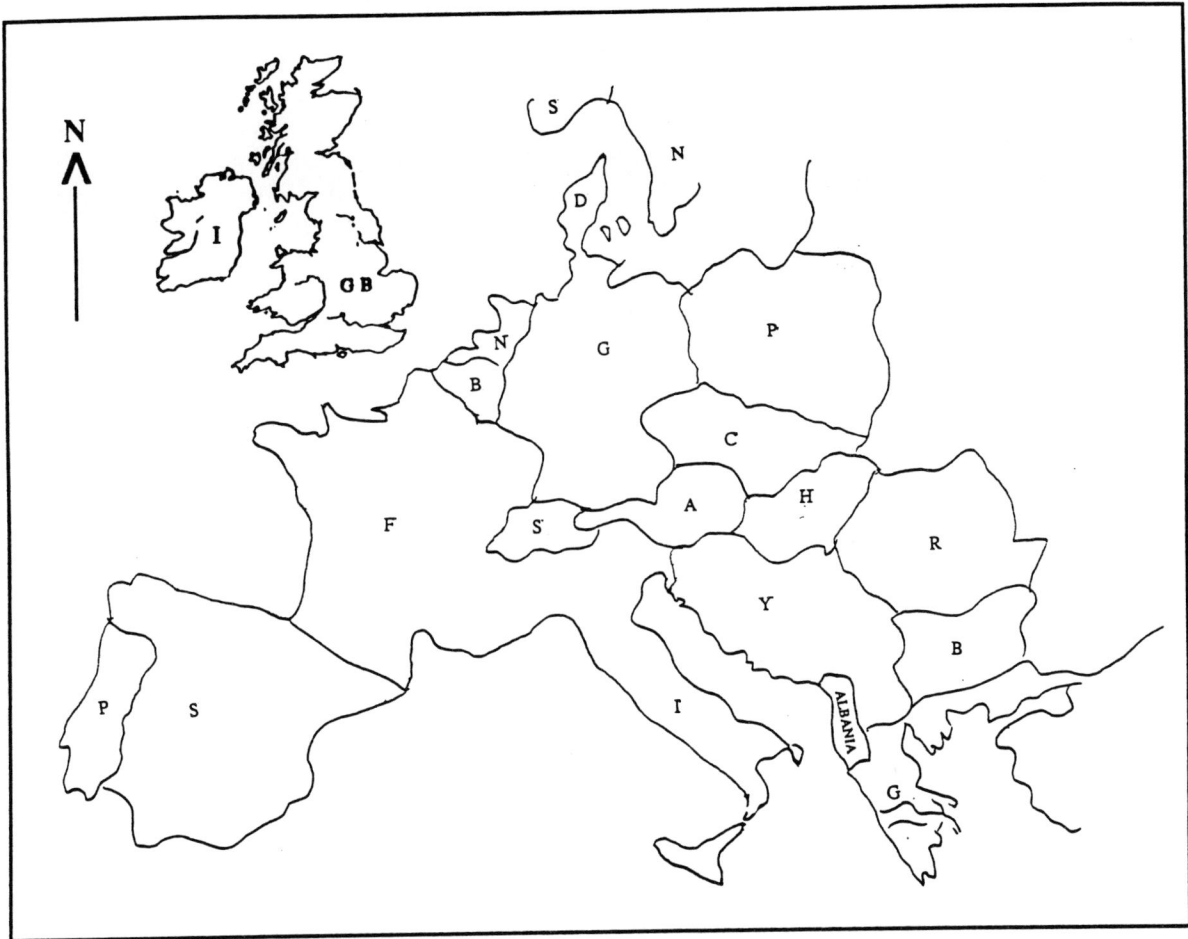

These are the countries which the Celts invaded or in which they settled.

ALBANIA,	GERMANY,	NORWAY,
AUSTRIA,	GREAT BRITAIN,	POLAND,
BELGIUM,	GREECE,	PORTUGAL,
BULGARIA,	HUNGARY,	RUMANIA,
CZECHOSLOVAKIA,	IRELAND,	SPAIN,
DENMARK,	ITALY,	SWEDEN,
FRANCE,	NETHERLANDS,	SWITZERLAND,
		*YUGOSLAVIA

Write their names on the map. The first one is done for you.

*Now BOSNIA

A CELTIC ROUNDHOUSE

How do you know this is a Celtic warrior's roundhouse?

How does the smoke from the fire escape?

Why was it quite dark inside a roundhouse even in the daytime?

What is the woman on the left doing?

How does this home differ from yours?

MAKE A CELTIC ROUNDHOUSE

Cut along dotted lines

Glue this sheet to cardboard and
cut out the pieces. Shape the circle
to form the roof. Bend and glue
the wall to the roof. Colour the
wall brown and add straw to
the roof for thatch.

BEND
AND GLUE

BEND

BEND
and GLUE

BEND

BEND
and GLUE

BEND

BEND
AND GLUE

BEND

A Celtic Roundhouse

A CELTIC VILLAGE

This is a Celtic village.

Look for the palisade. Why did the Celts build these?

What were roundhouses made of and how were they made weatherproof?

What are the men doing?

What are the women doing?

What does this picture tell you about how the Celts earned their living?

Draw a plan of a Celtic village.

Use your plan to make a model of a Celtic village.

FARMING

This is a Celtic farmer at work in his field.

The Celts had mixed farms. What does this mean?

The Celts were settled farmers, not nomadic. Why was this important and how did it affect the way they lived?

What are the advantages of living a settled life instead of a nomadic one?

Are there any disadvantages for the farmer?

FOOD

WHEAT   BARLEY

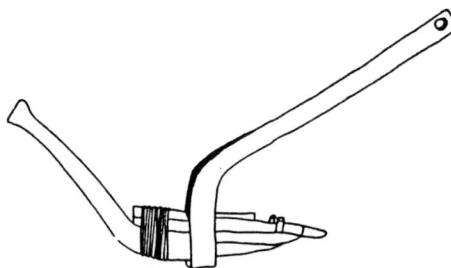

The plough used by the Celts was called an ard. It was pulled through the soil by two oxen.

The Celts ate meat especially at feasts. The farmers reared sheep, cows and pigs as well as chickens. Cereals were an important part of the Celts' diet and the farmers grew wheat and barley.

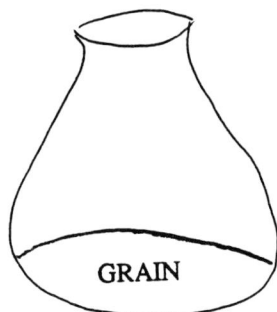

The storage pits of early man were shallow. Those dug by the Celts were big enough for a man to climb into them.

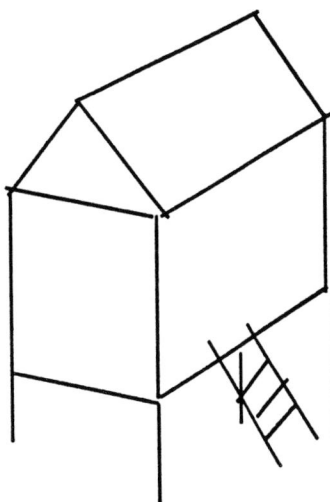

Air could circulate through the walls of the granary to dry the grain.

Grain was stored in pits below the ground and in wooden granaries above ground.

Grain was ground into flour to make bread using a quern.

Bread was baked in clay ovens.

The Celts used a quern (a handmill). This had two stones, the bottom one was fixed so that it could not move. The grain was fed through a hole or eye in the top stone. The stone was then ground by turning or rotating the top stone against the bottom one. The bottom stone had groves which allowed the flour to escape. The flour was gritty. It damaged the teeth of people who ate it, sometimes wearing the teeth down to the gums.

A CELTIC HILLFORT

This is a Celtic hillfort.

How did the Celts defend themselves?

Draw a plan of a Celtic hillfort. Use your plan to make a model of a hillfort.

A CELTIC WARRIOR

This is a Celtic warrior.

How did he make his hair 'stand up' in spikes? He also painted his body with woad. Why did he change his appearance in these ways?

A Celtic warrior had a special place in society. What was it?

ATTACKING A HILLFORT

These Celts are attacking an enemy's hillfort.

There are ten objects hidden in the picture. Find a mirror, a necklace, a pin, a torque, an armband, a bracelet, a brooch, mistletoe, a ring and a god.

A CELTIC CHIEFTAIN
Appearance, Dress and Arms

Swept back hair and drooping moustache. The moustache served as a strainer for wine and beer!

Large bronze helmets gave warriors extra height so they looked very tall. Sometimes there was the figure of a bird or an animal on top of the helmet.

Brooches (fibulae) were used to fasten cloaks at the breast or on the shoulder.

A torc or torque was worn around the neck. These were made of bronze, silver or gold. They were believed to be powerful charms and shock troops might go into battle naked except for their torcs to protect them from danger.

Leather belts were worn and many of these had decorative clasps.

Gold bracelets or armbands were worn. They were usually beautifully decorated.

Clothing. Celtic men wore trousers, tunics and cloaks. These were often brightly coloured and had checks like tartans.

Weapons. The Celts wore swords and daggers and often carried spears and shields. Many chieftains were buried with their weapons.

Celts used shields made of wood or leather to defend themselves. They were often long so as to cover most of the body.

Colour this Celtic chieftain. Paste him on cardboard and cut him out.

DRUIDS

Join the dots and find a sacred animal.

In this ceremony, a druid is cutting mistletoe. What happens in the rest of the ceremony?

Who were the druids and why were they important?

Did the Celts believe in one god or many?

WICKERMAN

This wooden monster was called a Wickerman. He was filled with humans who were then burnt alive.

It is probable that this monster did not exist but was invented by the Romans to discredit the Celts.

EXTRACTING AND WORKING IRON

The Celts were one of the first peoples to make and use iron in western Europe. A furnace is a special kind of fire. Early furnaces were shallow stone hearths which were filled with iron ore and charcoal. Air from bellows made the fire very hot (1,200°C). Molten iron was extracted from the ore. The Celts used deeper furnaces so that the liquid iron collected at the bottom and the waste or slag floated on top and could be skimmed off. Iron could be used to make tools and could be beaten into shape. Iron weapons such as daggers were stronger than bronze ones and had sharper edges.

CELTIC PATTERNS

Trace these Celtic patterns, colour them and use them to decorate a frame
for a picture or photograph.

CELTIC PATTERNS

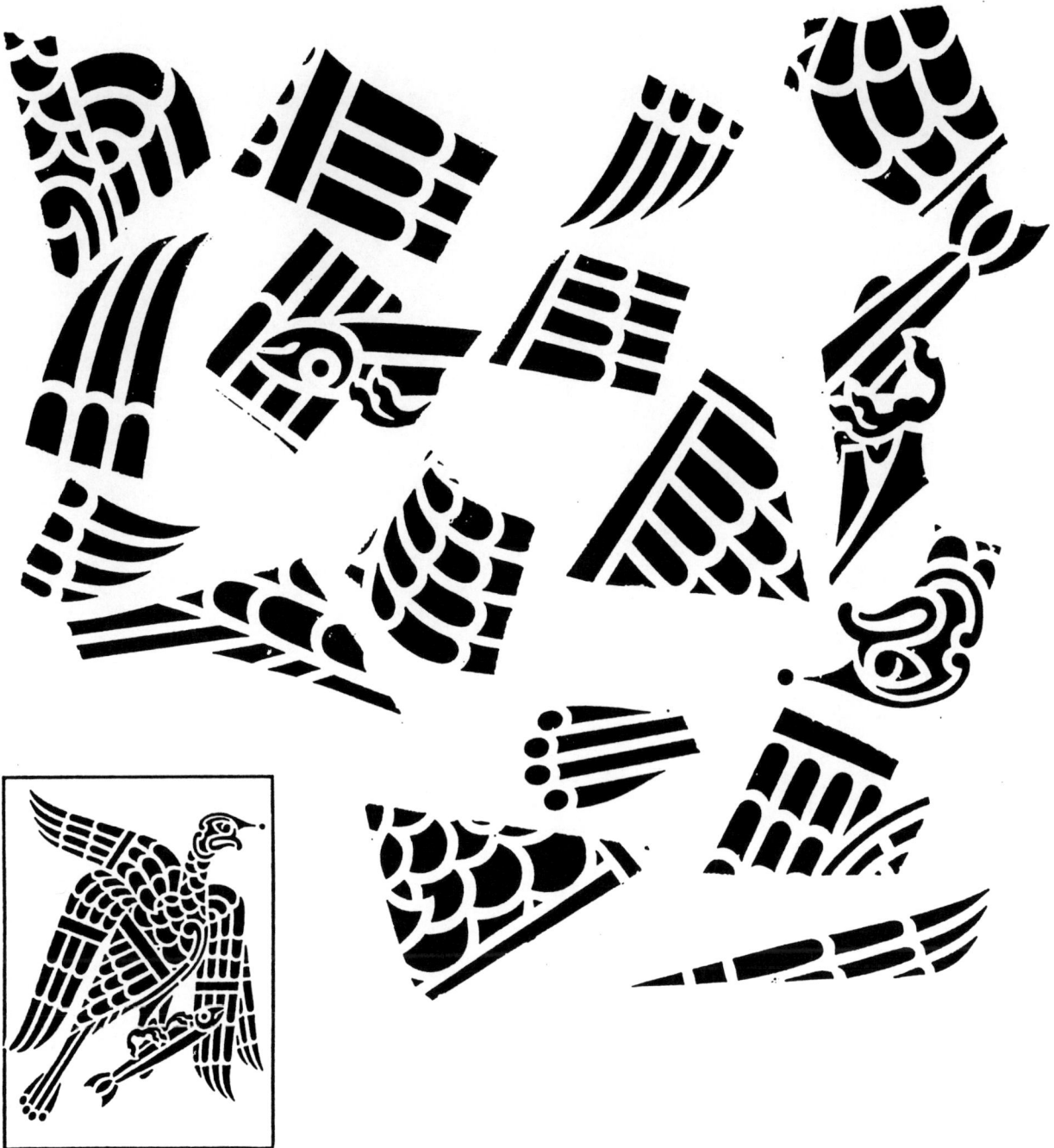

Trace and colour these pieces. Then cut them out and put them together to make this fantastic bird. What is the bird holding in its claws?

Cover the small bird with glitter and glue it to cardboard to make a Celtic brooch.

The Celts used brooches to fasten their clothes. Design a brooch using Celtic patterns that you would like to wear.

EVERYDAY LIFE OF A CELT

The following is a list of the tasks you might have to do if you lived at the time of the Celts. Use it to write an account of how you would live. How does it differ from the way you live today?

1. Get up when the sun wakes you.
2. Collect water from the stream for drinking and washing.
3. Sweep the floor.
4. Help prepare breakfast.
5. Feed the chickens.
6. Work in the field.
7. Dye yarn.
8. Weave cloth.
9. Polish father's helmet.
10. Decorate a new cooking pot.
11. Repair roof of your roundhouse.

Complete the following passage about the Celts by filling in the spaces:

The C . . . . lived about two thousand years ago in western E . . . . . including
B . . . . . . They lived in villages or s . . . . some of which grew into small
t . . . . They were skilled craftsmen and could make swords and weapons out of
i . . . . which was stronger than bronze. They lived in roundhouses made of wood
covered with d . . . The roofs were made of t . . . . . Meat and other food was
cooked in an iron c . . . . hung over a fire in the centre of the floor. Bread
was baked in a domed shaped clay o . . . The family worked as f . . . . . . They also
made pots and wove c . . . .

EARLY HISTORY TIMELINE

750 BC   The Celts settled in Britain

54 BC   The Romans arrived in Britain

2,000 BC   The Bronze Age

1,200 BC   The Celts, The Iron Age

6,000 BC   The New Stone Age

100,000 BC The Old Stone Age

Place these dates in the correct order.

A CELTIC DICTIONARY QUIZ

MEANING   WORD

1. A simple Celtic plough.

1

2. A warrior Queen.

2

3. Used by Celts to fasten their clothes - decorative.

3

4. Dye used by the Celts as war paint.

4

5. Kind of Celtic trumpet.

5

6. Most important Celt in a settlement.

6

7. Celtic priest.

7

8. A mixture of clay, straw, animal hair and dung used to make the walls of Celtic houses weatherproof.

8

9. A Celtic fortress.

9

10. Fence around a settlement built as a defence against attack.

10

11. A Celtic house.

11

12. Necklace worn by Celtic men and women.

12

Fill in the boxes.

The Celts Master File © EJP & DCP

THE CELTIC NEWS

You are a special correspondent with *The Celtic News*, a leading newspaper. Remember to illustrate all your reports and stories with drawings, paintings or cartoons.

1. **As a wartime reporter, you have been asked to go with a band of Celtic warriors on a raid on a neighbouring hillfort and write an eyewitness account of the battle.**

[Remember to include the preparations for battle, the reasons for the raid, the journey to the hillfort, the timing of the raid - at sunrise or undercover of darkness, battle plans (may be secret), noise, smells, fear and excitement of battle, how long the battle lasts and how it ends, number of injured and dead, return journey. . .]

2. **Write a letter to your parents or a friend from the battle lines.**

3. **When the battle is over and the victorious chieftain returns to his village, you are expected to interview him personally.**

[This is an exclusive inverview. Personal details are needed including picture (drawing) of the chieftain, his name, age, where he was born and grew up, family (were his sons in the raiding party?). Reasons for the battle, his role and reactions to the success. His views on the relationship between his men and the conquered settlement. . .]

4. **The next day you are to visit the conquered hillfort and interview the people who live there.**

[Describe the scene of devastation - noise, smells, colours, atmosphere. What are the people doing - repairs, wandering aimlessly? Interview a man, a woman and a child. How did they survive the attack? How will the settlement recover? Is a revenge attack planned or likely?]

THE WARRIOR QUEEN

Win the battle or perish. That is what I, a woman, intend to do.
Let the men live in slavery if they wish.

Recorded by the Roman historian, Tacitus, writing about Boadicea

Boadicea (or Boudicca) was queen of the Iceni, a Celtic tribe who lived in eastern England (now called Norfolk). She did not have a son and when her husband, King Prasutagus, died in AD 60, he left his property to be shared between his two daughters. The Roman emperor, Nero, was also given a share because Prasutagus wished for Roman protection for his family. However, the Romans in Britain plundered the kingdom and ill-treated Boadicea.

The Iceni were furious. Led by the warlike Boadicea, they and most of East Anglia rebelled against the Romans. Boadicea and her two daughters rode in a chariot with knife-blades on its axles. The Celts captured and destroyed the Roman strongholds of Camulodunum (Colchester), Verulam (St Albans), the Mart of Londinium (London) and several military posts. More than 70,000 Romans and those Britons who had befriended them were slaughtered. The Ninth Roman Legion marched from Lincoln to their rescue but was cut to pieces by the all conquering Celts.

Their triumph was short-lived. Suetonius Paulinus, the Roman governor of Britain, hurried to the rescue of his troops. At first he could do little. Then he carefully chose a new battleground at Fenny Stratford in Buckinghamshire where he knew he would have military advantage. Boadicea drove her chariot along the Celtic battle lines, urging her soldiers on but the trained legionaries were too powerful and better organised. In a desperate battle, thousands of her brave followers were slaughtered. In despair, when Boadicea realised all was lost, she took poison.

Answer the following questions.

1. Name a coin on which Boadicea appears today. Draw a picture of her.

2. Write one word to describe Boadicea. What Celtic tribe did Boadicea lead?

3. Why did Boadicea revolt against the Romans?

4. What relatives accompanied Boadicea on her mission to conquer the Romans?

5. Name three places Boadicea and her followers conquered. According to the passage, how many Romans and their friends were killed?

6. Name the Roman Legion who first fought against Boadicea. What happened to it?

7. Name the Roman governor of Britain in AD 60.

8. What happened at Fenny Stratford?

9. Why did Boadicea kill herself?

10. Give the meaning of property, protection, plundered, ill-treated, warlike, strongholds, befriended, powerful, slaughtered, trained, desperate, despair.

11. Draw a battle scene between Boadicea and her followers and the Romans.

12. Imagine you are Boadicea. Write an account of your exploits beginning . . . My name is Boadicea and I am Queen of the Iceni, a Celtic tribe living in Eastern England . . .

THE CELTIC LEGACY

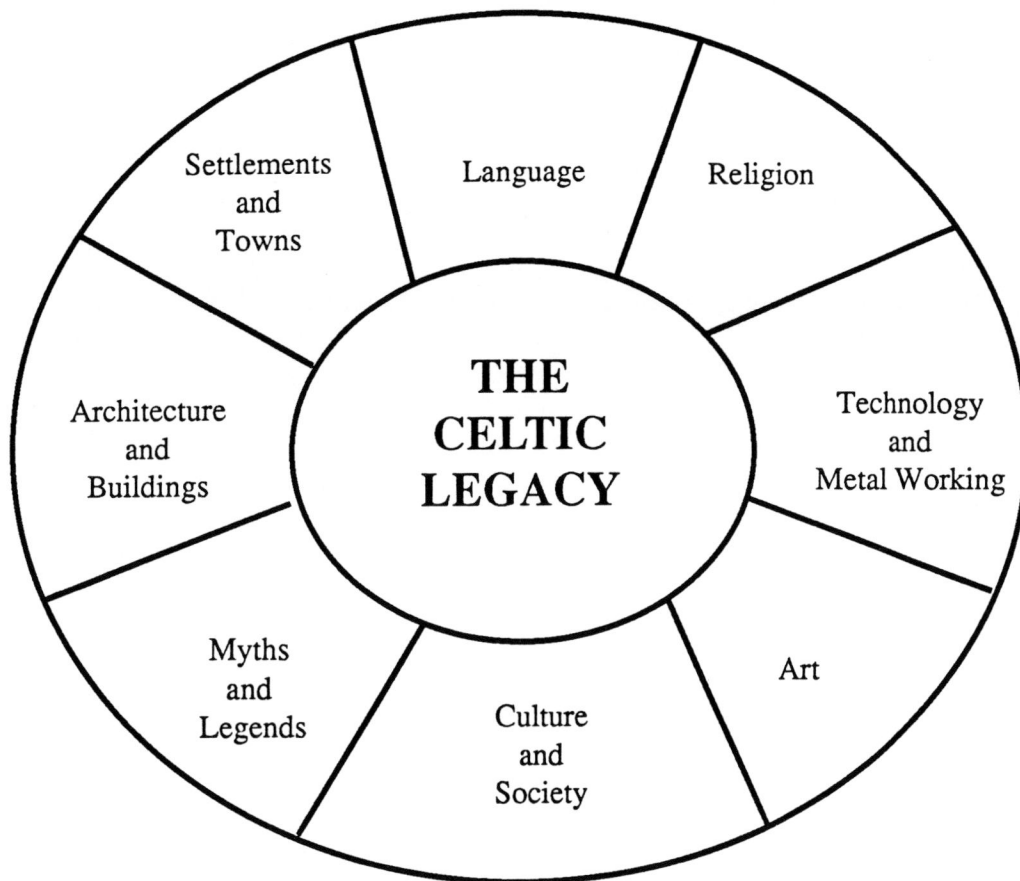

. Make this Celtic Legacy Wheel the centre of a Celtic Legacy Wall.
Draw and colour pictures for each part.

[Some suggestions:

1. Settlements and towns - draw a Celtic village. Name present day places and towns that grew from Celtic settlements. When Celtic settlements were taken over by the Romans, some of them became important Roman provincial towns.

2. Buildings - draw a roundhouse and a hillfort.

3. Language - Mark the countries on a map where the people speak Celtic languages.

4. Art - The Celts decorated pots and pans, that is useful as well as ornamental items. Draw pots with Celtic patterns.

5. Culture - at first poetry from the druids was not written down and was passed on by word of mouth. It was spoken at gatherings. Its lyrical quality is found in today's Celtic languages.

6. Folk customs - gatherings such as the Eisteddfodau in Wales and the Highland Games in Scotland may be linked to the Celts. Also clans under the leadership of lairds (chieftains) in Scotland have much in common with the organisation of Celtic tribes.

7. Folklore and superstitions of some Gaelic peoples have links with the Celts, for example, the use of mistletoe.]

BARTER

BROOCH

POT

IRON DAGGER

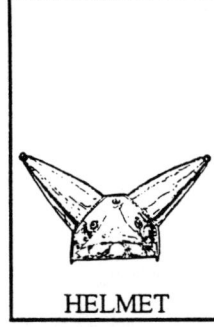

HELMET

SHEEP

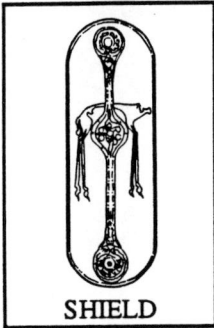

SHIELD

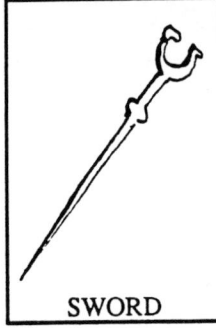

SWORD

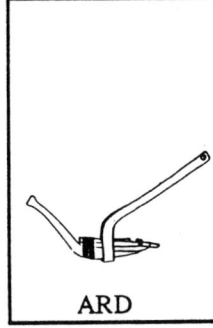

ARD

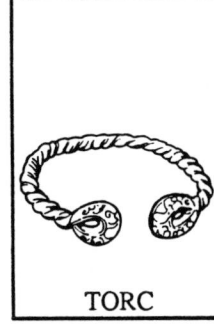

TORC

CHICKENS

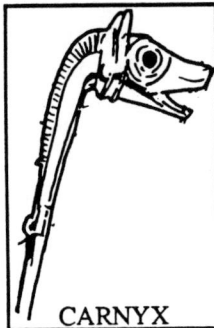

CARNYX

FIRE-DOGS and CAULDRON

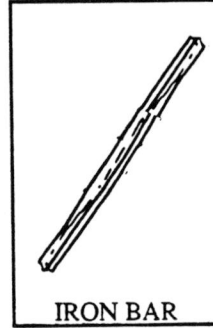

IRON BAR

QUERN

SPEAR

CHARIOT

SOME EARLY COINS

Glue them on to card and cut them out and use them to trade.

The Celts used coins in Britain just before the Romans came. Before there were coins, they traded by barter, that is they exchanged some goods for others. For example, an iron bar might be worth a sheep while a small sack of grain might be exchanged for a chicken or a dozen eggs. Colour these pictures and glue the sheet on to cardboard. Cut out the cards and set up a market stall. Traders have cards they wish to exchange for goods (cards) brought by the customers. It may be difficult to decide who is the better off at the end and therefore the winner. Set a time limit because bartering and haggling (arguing over the value of different goods) can take a long time. Draw any Celtic picture you like on the blank card.

AN ARCHAEOLOGICAL DIG

List the special equipment these young archaeologists are using. Why are they wearing safety helmets?

An archaeologist is examining a site thought to be that of a Celtic settlement. Which of the following might he or she expect to find? (Answer yes/no/maybe.)

Skin, hair, bones, teeth, plastic buttons, leather tops of shoes, plastic purse, coins, iron axe head, broken pieces of pottery, bronze knife, amber, gold torc, gold buckle, spectacles, ball point pen, watch, aluminium can, a bronze beaker.

Explain to a friend who knows nothing about history or archaeology why trying to find the remains of a Celtic settlement is interesting and worthwhile.

Which of the following does an archaeologist do?

1. Examine remains found underground or under water.
2. Collect evidence from ploughed fields - field walking.
3. Make detailed plans of a site.
4. Collect broken pottery and bones.
5. Check finds against records.
6. Prepare a report and/or exhibition on his or her work.
7. Take aerial photographs.
8. Investigate 'humps' and 'lumps' in fields.
9. Investigate differences in the growth of vegetation in fields.
10. Examine teeth.
11. Take fingerprints.
12. Examine cloth.
13. Flatten a site to make digging easier.
14. Use a bulldozer to make excavation quicker.

PUZZLES

1. Which path must the warrior follow to get to his roundhouse?

2. Which piece has broken off the cauldron?

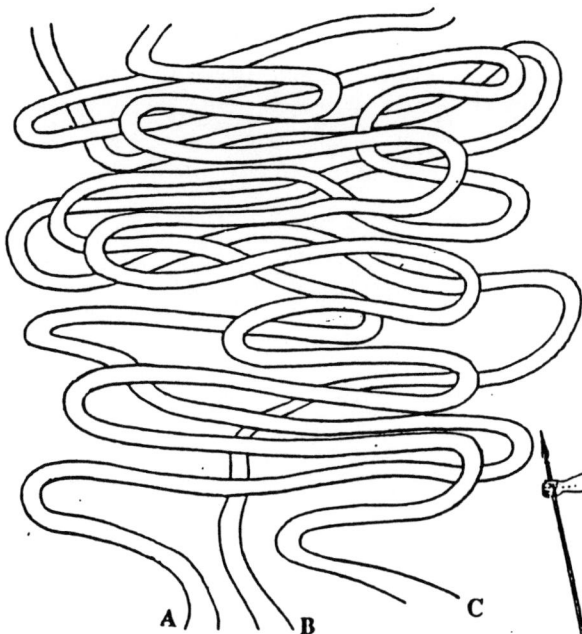

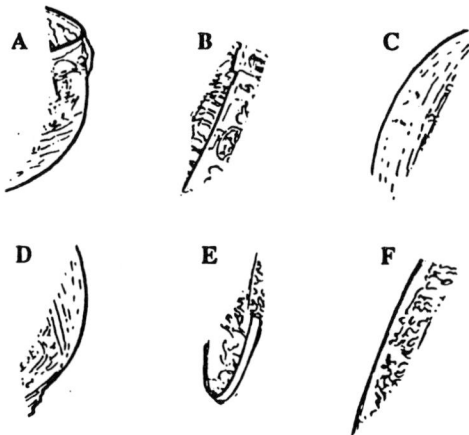

A   B   C

D   E   F

A   B   C

3. Which two shields are exactly the same?

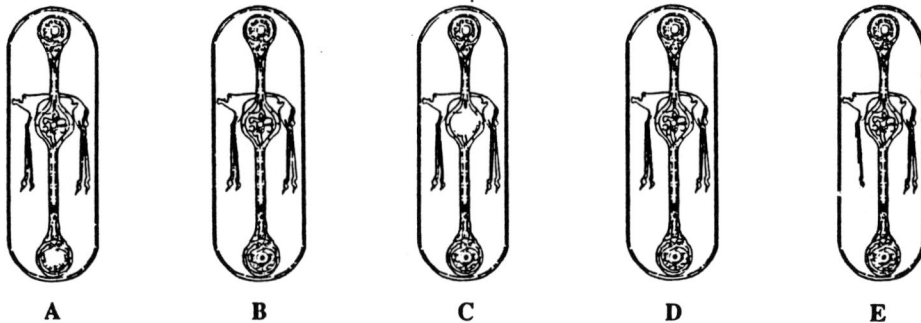

A   B   C   D   E

4. Place these wine flagons in order of size beginning with the smallest and ending with the biggest. Which one is the same size as the flagon in the square?

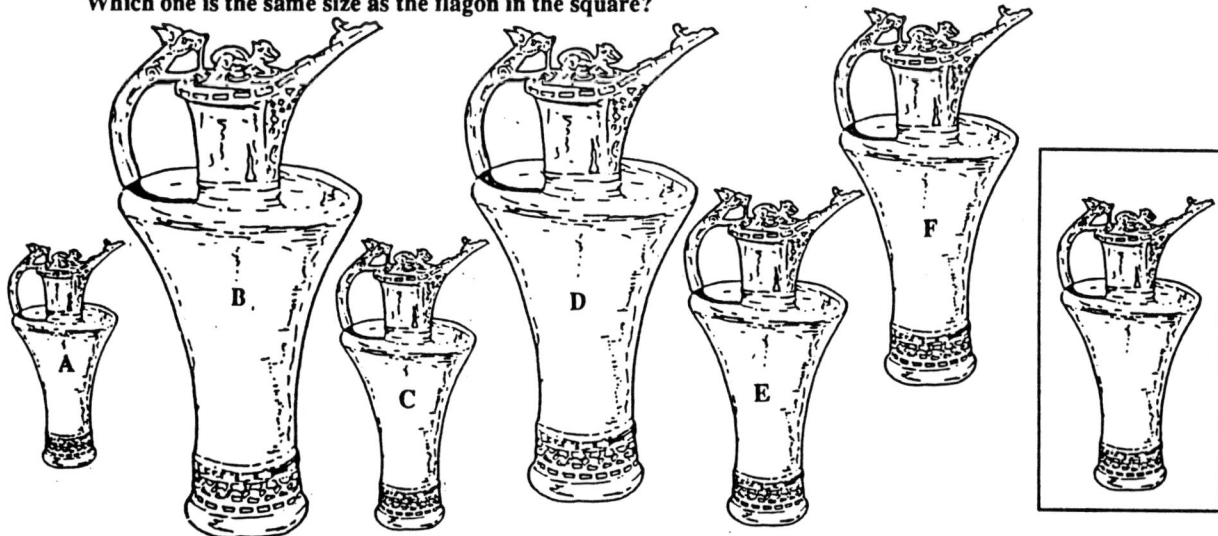

PUZZLES

Find ten differences between these pictures of Celtic women preparing food inside a roundhouse then colour the pictures.

PUZZLES

1. The following are clues to words hidden in the word square. Can you find them?
The words may be in the square backwards, upside down or diagonally and any letter may be used more than once.

T	T	R	I	B	E	H	W	O	A	D	B	R
R	R	O	T	O	R	C	A	A	A	R	R	O
O	U	M	E	A	D	B	R	Y	S	E	O	U
F	M	E	M	T	R	P	R	E	D	H	O	N
E	P	N	L	E	U	D	I	R	U	B	C	D
I	E	E	E	B	I	R	O	N	N	U	H	H
H	T	D	H	T	D	W	R	O	G	A	S	O
C	H	A	L	K	S	H	I	E	L	D	T	U
G	O	D	S	P	A	L	I	S	A	D	E	S
T	F	A	R	M	E	R	S	R	A	W	N	E

1. Worn on the head.
2. Worn around the neck.
3. Drunk by the Celts.
4. Celtic priests.
5. Blown in battle.
6. Celts were the first to extract this metal.
7. Brave Celt who fought battles.
8. Used to keep clothing together.
9. Carried for protection in a battle.
10. A sign of bad luck or good luck.
11. Long weapon.
12. City sacked by the Celts.
13. Blue vegetable dye.
14. Head of a settlement.
15. Celts put this on their hair before battle.
16. Simple plough.
17. To rear cattle, especially young ones.
18. Used to weatherproof Celtic houses.
19. Lays eggs.
20. Defensive fence around a Celtic settlement.
21. Most Celts were . . . .
22. Battles.
23. Worshipped by the Celts.
24. Makes honey.
25. Clan.
26. Celtic home.
27. Decorative pin.
28. Father.
29. Celts built this at the top of a hill.
30. Used to travel on water.
31. Boiled boar.
32. Grain was laid on trays to . . .
33. Fodder from grass.
34. Part of daub.
35. To chafe.
36. Group of cattle.
37. Bright, decorative colour.
38. Used to catch fish.
39. Celts lived a long time . . .
40. Not night.
41. One more than nine.
42. Useful if 30 sinks.

2. Who am I?

My first is in war but not in battle.
My second is in palisade but not in fence.
My third is in fire and also in water.
My fourth is in spear and also in fear.
My fifth is in shield but not in sword.
My sixth is in foe but not in enemy.
My last is found twice in chariot.
My whole is a hero of the Celts.

3. The following are the names of things you might find in a Celtic settlement but the letters are muddled up. What are they?

ARAYNGR, YETROTP, HLGUPO, TPIS, RATC, ETSILOMET, OMLO, PRASE, RDLUNOAC, RTHOACI.

4. How many words can you make from the letters in

A CELTIC SETTLEMENT?

(30 words good, 60 words very good, 100 words excellent.)

A CELTIC QUIZ

1. Who were the Celts?

2. Where did the word 'Celt' come from and what did it mean?

3. When did the Celts first arrive in Britain?

4. Where did the word 'Britons' come from?

5. What part of Britain did the Celts occupy?

6. What shape were Celtic houses and what were they called?

7. What were Celtic houses made of?

8. How were Celtic houses heated?

9. What is the name of the fence around a Celtic settlement?

10. The Celts were important because they were one of the first invaders to settle in Britain. What was their main occupation?

11. What did Celtic farmers produce?

12. What is an ard?

13. What skill more than any other separated the Celts from earlier people?

14. Name the five levels of Celtic society.

15. What was the name given to Celtic priests?

16. What were Celtic musicians and poets called?

17. Stone and bronze were used before Celtic times. What new material did the Celts learn to extract and use?

18. Celtic warriors decorated their bodies with a blue dye. From which plant was this obtained?

19. Many Celtic warriors fought naked in battle. Why?

20. Name a famous Celtic queen who led the Iceni.

21. The Celts had no buttons to fasten their clothes. What did they use?

22. What is a torc or torque?

23. Give the name of the Celtic long trumpet.

24. Name (a) the bull or ram horned god, (b) the horse goddess.

25. Name the plant associated with sacrifices and which the Celts thought sacred.

26. What shows that the Celts believed in afterlife?

27. Name the famous place in Dorset where Celtic remains have been discovered [M . . . . . C . . . . .]

28. Name the marsh in North Wales where a famous Celtic hoard was found. [L . . . C . . . . . B . . . Anglesey]

29. Name the four main Celtic festivals.

30. Identify the following objects.

A

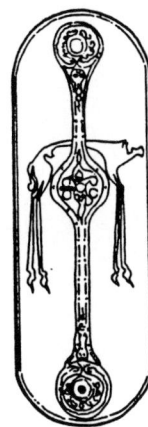

B

C

D

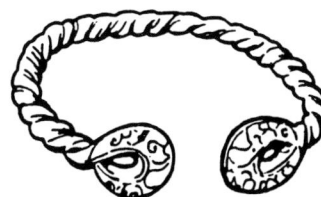

E

CARD GAMES
PICK A LETTER
For two or more players.

Paste the letter sheet on to card and cut out the squares. Place them face down on the table. The card ? can be any letter. There are two ways in which the game can be played, one is a little simpler than the other.

QUICK AND SIMPLE

Each player turns over a letter until he or she can make a word. The word is then picked up and placed in front of the player. Score 1 point for each letter in the word. The other players (One after the other) continue to turn over the letter cards. The game finishes when all the cards have been turned over and the player with the most points wins.

For example: Suppose Player 1 turns over letter A. Player 2 turns over letter T.

Player 3 turns over letter F and makes the word FAT scoring 3 points and placing the word in front of him or her.

A LITTLE HARDER

If you wish you may also use words already made by you or other players.

Suppose Player 4 turns over Letter E, takes the word FAT and makes FATE scoring 4 points and placing the word in front of him or her.

Player 1 turns over the letter S and takes the letters FATE and makes FEAT (4 points) then FEATS, then FATES, then FEAST scoring 4 + 5 + 5 + 5 = 19 points.

You can of course make extra letter cards to make the game last longer. Only words found in a good dictionary can be accepted. [Rules can vary, for example, smallest word accepted must have four letters, no plurals allowed. You may decide to award say 10 bonus points for words on a 'Celtic' list such as Celt, torc, and ard . . . Agree how the game is to be played before you start.]

NB If the letters of a word can be re-arranged to make another word then it is an ANAGRAM. Therefore FEAT is an anagram of FATE.

CELTIC SNAP

For two or more players.

You need four copies of the picture card sheet and the backing sheet of roundhouses. Colour the picture cards so that the ones with the same picture are coloured alike. Paste the sheets on cardboard and cut out the cards. **You will have four of each kind - four Celtic chieftains, four warriors and so on.** There is a roundhouse picture for the back of each card.

Shuffle the cards and deal them all out face down. The players hold their cards face down so that they cannot be seen. The player to the left of the dealer places a card face up on the table. In turn, each player places a card face up on top of this. When two cards with the same picture follow each other, the player who first shouts SNAP picks up the cards on the table. The winner is the one with all the cards.

MIX AND MATCH

The aim of the game is to find pairs of identical pictures. The pack of cards is shuffled and the dealer lays out the pack face down on a table or on the floor. The person to the left of the dealer turns over two cards. If they are the same, he or she keeps them and has another turn, if not the cards are turned face down again. The person to the left then picks up two cards and so on. As more cards are turned over and replaced, it is possible to remember which are pairs. The winner is the player with the most pairs. This can also be played by one person who sets a target time by which all the cards must be paired.

A	A	A	B	B	C
C	D	D	E	E	E
E	F	G	H	I	I
J	K	L	M	M	N
N	O	O	O	P	Q
R	S	S	T	U	U
V	W	X	Y	Z	?

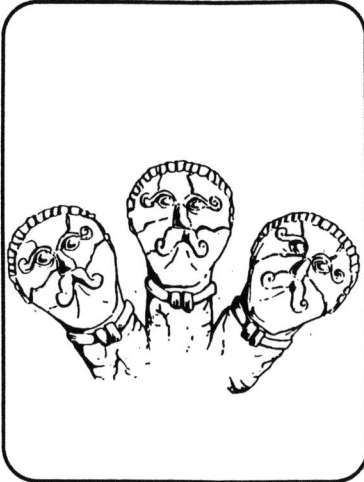
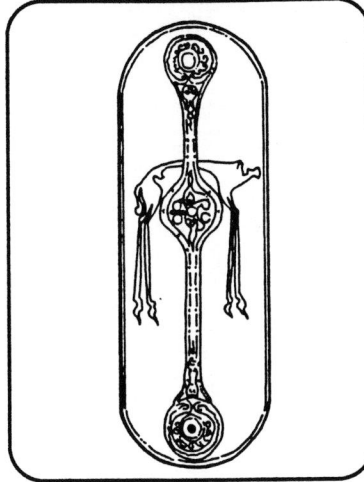

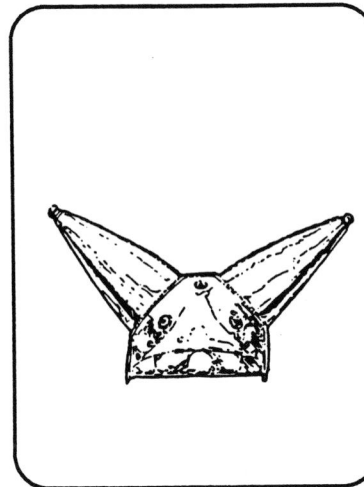

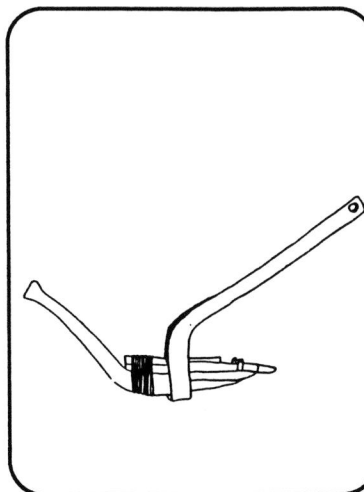

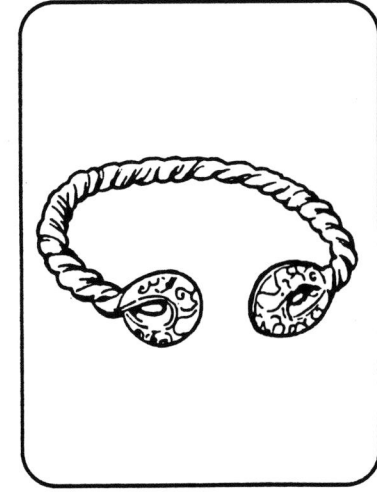

The Celts Master File © EJP & DCP

CELEBRATE VICTORY

31 Help to prepare feast. Have another turn. **32**

Work on a new torc for chief. Go to 35. **33**

Chief returns wounded from battle. Go back to 17. **34**

35

Warriors return victorious. Have another turn. **30**

Help with weaving Go to 31. **29**

28

Unlucky omen from gods. Go back to 17 and miss a turn. **27**

26

Use wrong colour dye for yarn. Miss a turn. **25**

Plough breaks on stone. Go back to 19. **24**

23

22

Use cart to carry grain. Have another turn. **15**

Put grain to dry in granaries. Have another turn. **16**

17

Feed pigs. Go to 21. **18**

19

Drink too much mead. Fall asleep and fail to do tasks. Go back to 8. **20**

Help Druid cut mistletoe. Go to 28. **21**

14

Repair broken palisade. Go to 17. **13**

12

Cook meal. Have another turn. **11**

Go hunting and get lost. Go back to 4. **10**

Repair broken spear heads and swords. Have another turn. **9**

8

Work on a helmet for the chief. Go to 17. **7**

START

Warriors prepare for war. Miss a turn. **1**

2

Make a sacrifice to the gods for father's safe return from battle. Have another turn. **3**

4

6

Blow carnyx. Have another turn. **5**

It is 650 BC and you live in a Celtic village and your father is the chieftain.
Colour the game sheet including the figures. Glue it on to cardboard. Cut out the figures and bend the supports at the bottom to make them stand up. You need a die*.
Put the figures at the start. The player to throw the highest number starts then the player with the next highest number and so on. In the game, move the figures the number of squares indicated by the die.
The first player to join in the feasting is the winner.
*NB The plural of die is dice.

Cut — Cut — Cut — Cut

BEND — BEND — BEND — BEND

PROJECT IDEAS

1. Celtic Life.
2. Battle Plans in Celtic Times.
3. Celtic Dress.
4. Food and Cooking in Celtic Times.
5. Farming in Celtic Times.
6. Celtic Art.
7. The Art of Defence in Celtic Times.
8. Religion and the Druids.
9. Celtic Superstitions and Customs.
10. The Celtic Legacy.
11. Metal Working in Celtic Times.
12. Celtic Weapons.
13. Celtic Sites and Archaeology Today.
14. Celtic Hoards and Treasures and Their Importance.
15. Celtic Burials.
16. Celtic Society and Class Structure.
17. Women in Celtic Society.
18. Boadicea (Boudicca).
19. Investigation of a Local Celtic Site.
20. Why we should investigate the Past.

THINGS TO MAKE

1. A model of a Celtic roundhouse.
2. A model of a Celtic village.
3. A model of a Celtic hillfort.
4. A Celtic bookmark.
5. A Celtic paperweight (paint a Celtic warrior on a smooth pebble or shell.)
6. A Celtic Brooch.
7. A Desk Tidy decorated with Celtic pictures.
8. A Tidy Box decorated with Celtic pictures.
9. A Celtic Frieze of Celtic pictures.
10. Puppets of Celtic characters for a puppet play.

ANSWERS

Page 21
See map on page 7.

Page 36
The Celts lived about two thousand years ago in western Europe including Britain. They lived in villages or settlements some of which grew into small towns. They were skilled craftsmen and could make swords and weapons out of iron which was stronger than bronze. They lived in roundhouses made of wood covered with daub. The roofs were made of thatch. Meat and other food was cooked in an iron cauldron hung over a fire in the centre of the floor. Bread was baked in a domed shaped clay oven. The family worked as farmers. They also made pots and wove cloth.

Page 37
Ard, Boadicea, brooch, woad, carnyx, chieftain, druid, daub, hillfort, palisade, roundhouse, torc.

Page 42
Yes: bones, teeth, a bronze beaker, coins, iron axe head, broken pieces of pottery, bronze knife, amber, gold torc, gold buckle.
No: Skin, plastic buttons, leather tops of shoes, plastic purse, spectacles, ball point pen, watch, aluminium can.
Maybe: Hair.

An archaeologist might carry out the following: 1, 2, 3 ,4, 5, 6, 7, 8, 9, 10, 12.

Page 43
1 C. 2 D. 3 B and D. 4 A C E F D B. Flagon C is the same size as the one in the square.

Page 44

Page 45   **1. Word square.**

1. Helmet.	15. Chalkwash.	29. Fort.
2. Torc.	16. Ard.	30. Boat.
3. Mead.	17. Breed.	31. Ham.
4. Druids.	18. Daub.	32. Dry.
5. Trumpet.	19. Hen.	33. Hay.
6. Iron.	20. Palisade.	34. Dung.
7. Warrior.	21. Farmers.	35. Rub.
8. Pin.	22. Wars.	36. Herd.
9. Shield.	23. Gods.	37. Red.
10. Omen.	24. Bee.	38. Nets.
11. Sword.	25. Tribe.	39. Ago.
12. Rome.	26. Roundhouse.	40. Day.
13. Woad.	27. Brooch.	41. Ten.
14. Chief.	28. Dad.	42. Raft.

2. WARRIOR.
3. GRANARY, POTTERY, PLOUGH, SPIT, CART, MISTLETOE, LOOM, SPEAR, CAULDRON, CHARIOT.

Page 46 Quiz
1. A race of people who invaded and settled in Europe about 650 BC.
2. From the Greek 'Keltoi' meaning a warlike people.
3. About 500 BC or before.
4. From the Celtic tribe known as Prythons.
5. Most of Britain south of the Scottish Highlands.
6. Mainly round. They were called roundhouses.
7. Wood, reeds, hardened dung and mud with thatched roofs of reed and straw.
8. By a fire (a hearth) in the centre of the floor.
9. Palisade.
10. Mixed farming.
11. They grew crops and reared cattle.
12. A simple plough.
13. The Celts could make things from iron.
14. Chieftain, druids, nobles, freemen/farmers and landless/slaves.
15. Druids.
16. Bards.
17. Iron.
18. Woad plant.
19. They believed that not wearing clothes gave them super-human power. Their wild appearance was intended to frighten and shock their enemies.
20. Boadicea or Boudicca.
21. Decorated brooches and pins.
22. A neckband or necklace made of bronze, silver or gold.
23. Carnyx.
24. (a) Cernunnos (b) Epona.
25. Mistletoe.
26. They filled the graves of their chieftains and warriors with goods to use in the underworld.
27. Maiden Castle.
28. Llyn Cerrig Bach.
29. Beltane, Imbolc, Lughnasa, Samain.
30. A Wine flagon, B Shield, C Pin, D Long Trumpet (carnyx), E Torc or torque.

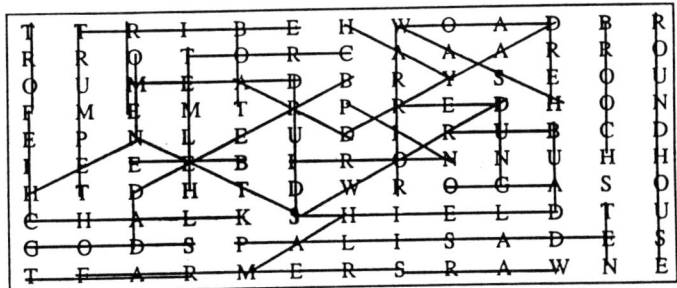

RECORD SHEET
INVADERS AND SETTLERS
THE CELTS

Name _____   Age _____

Page	Master Copy
21	Countries Celts Invaded
22	A Celtic Roundhouse
23	Make A Celtic Roundhouse
24	A Celtic Village
25	Farming
26	Food
27	A Celtic Hillfort
28	A Celtic Warrior
29	Attacking a Hillfort
30	A Celtic Chieftain
31	Druids
32	Wickerman
33	Extracting and Working Iron
34	Celtic Patterns
35	Celtic Patterns
36	Everyday Life of a Celt
37	Early History Timeline
37	A Celtic Dictionary Quiz
38	*The Celtic News*
39	The Warrior Queen (Boadicea)
40	The Celtic Legacy
41	Barter
42	An Archaeological Dig
43/45	Puzzles
46	A Celtic Quiz
47	Rules for Card Games
48	Pick A Letter Game
49	Celtic Snap
50	Celtic Game
51	Project List
52	Things to Make

MASTER FILES
ORDER FORM

KEY STAGE 1 (Age 5 - 7)　　**KEY STAGE 2 (Age 7 - 11)**　　**KEY STAGE 3 (Age 11 - 14)**

Quantity	Title	ISBN	Price	Cost
	KS1 ENGLISH	1 85772 111 X	£20.00	£
	KS1 MATHEMATICS	1 85772 107 1	£20.00	£
	KS1 MENTAL MATHEMATICS	1 85772 154 3	£20.00	£
	KS1 SCIENCE	1 85772 108 X	£20.00	£
	KS1 HISTORY	1 85772 112 8	£20.00	£
	KS2 ENGLISH	1 85772 085 7	£20.00	£
	KS2 MATHEMATICS	1 85772 086 5	£20.00	£
	KS2 SCIENCE	1 85772 087 3	£20.00	£
	KS3 ENGLISH	1 85772 127 6	£20.00	£
	KS3 MATHEMATICS	1 85772 126 8	£20.00	£
	KS3 SCIENCE	1 85772 128 4	£20.00	£
HISTORY				
	KS2 Invaders and Settlers, The Celts	1 85772 067 9	£15.95	£
	KS2 Invaders and Settlers, The Romans	1 85772 070 9	£15.95	£
	KS2 Invaders and Settlers, The Vikings	1 85772 069 5	£15.95	£
	KS2 Life in Tudor Times	1 85772 076 8	£15.95	£
	KS2/KS3 Victorian Britain	1 85772 077 6	£15.95	£
TOPICS				
	KS2/KS3 Castles	1 85772 075 X	£15.95	£
	CHRISTMAS (AGES 5 - 12)	1 85772 065 2	£20.00	£
NEW FOR EARLY YEARS				
	First Steps Basic Activities in the 3Rs	1 85772 130 6	£12.50	£
	First Steps Number and Counting	1 85772 133 0	£12.50	£
	First Steps Beginning to Read	1 85772 138 1	£12.50	£
	First Steps Beginning to Write	1 85772 139 X	£12.50	£
	First Steps Beginning Mental Maths	1 85772 142 X	£12.50	£
	First Steps Mental Maths, 5 - 6 years	1 85772 143 8	£12.50	£
	First Steps Mental Maths, 6 - 7 years	1 85772 146 2	£12.50	£
	First Steps Mental Maths, 7 - 8 years	1 85772 147 0	£12.50	£
	First Steps Mental Maths 8 - 9 years	1 85772 148 9	£12.50	£
	First Steps Developing Literacy Skills 4 - 5 years	1 85772 151 9	£12.50	£
	First Steps Developing Literacy Skills 5- 6 years	1 85772 152 7	£12.50	£
	First Steps Developing Literacy Skills 6 - 7 years	1 85772 153 5	£12.50	£
	Reading and Comprehension 5 - 7 years, Book 1	1 85772 144 6	£12.50	£
	Reading and Comprehension 5 - 7 years, Book 2	1 85772 145 4	£12.50	£

Name/Organisation/School	Total	£

Address

Post Code　　　　Tel.

Contact　　Signature

Order Number　　　　Date

Available from Blackwells, Foyles Bookshop, Waterstones, Welsh Books Council, WH Smith, and all good booksellers or direct from

DOMINO BOOKS (WALES) LTD, P O BOX 32, SWANSEA SA1 1 FN.
Tel. 01792 459378　Fax. 01792 466337

All official orders must have an official requisition form attached (schools, educational establishments, LEAs, bookshops, libraries). Cheques with private orders please.